"The pleasures of the table
are common to all ages and ranks,
to all countries and times: they not only
harmonize with all the other pleasures,
but remain to console us
for their loss."

— Anthèlme de Brillat-Savarin

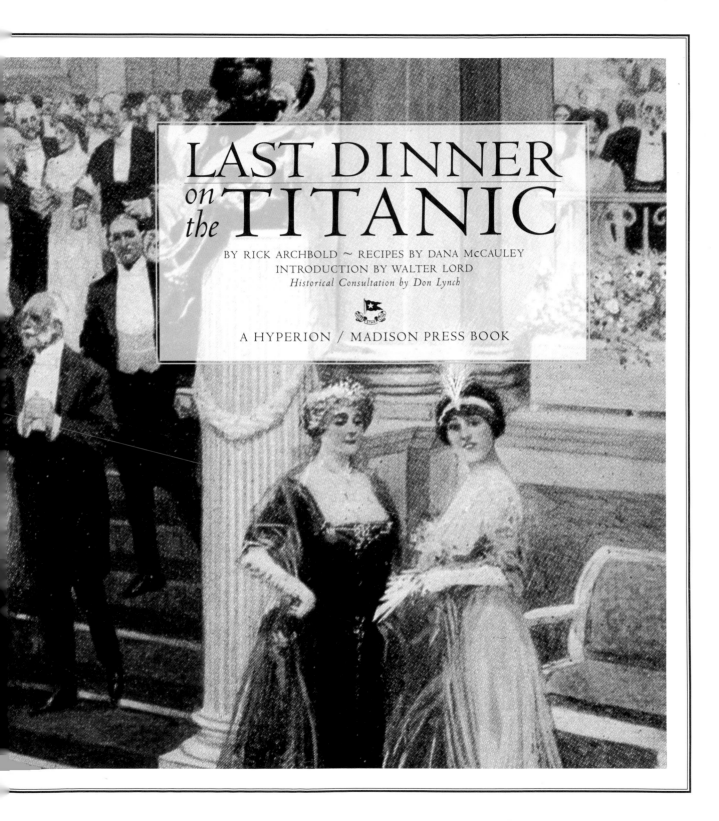

LAST DINNER
on *the* TITANIC

BY RICK ARCHBOLD ~ RECIPES BY DANA McCAULEY
INTRODUCTION BY WALTER LORD
Historical Consultation by Don Lynch

A HYPERION / MADISON PRESS BOOK

To the memory of all those who prepared and served the food aboard the R.M.S. Titanic.

Library of Congress Cataloging-in-Publication Data

Archbold, Rick. 1950 —
Last dinner on the Titanic : menus and recipes from the legendary
liner / text by Rick Archbold : recipes by Dana McCauley.
p.   cm.
Includes bibliographical references and index.
ISBN 0-7868-6303-X
I. Cookery.   2. Titanic (Steamship)   I. McCauley, Dana.   II. Title
TX652.A737   1997   96–47057
641.5'753—dc21   CIP

First Edition
10 9 8 7 6 5 4 3

Produced by
Madison Press Books
40 Madison Avenue, Toronto, Ontario
Canada M5R 2S1

Printed and bound in Great Britain

"It was a brilliant assembly — contentment and happiness prevailed."

— First-class passenger Elmer Taylor

Contents

Foreword

EIGHTY-FIVE YEARS AFTER HER SINKING, THE *TITANIC* ENCHANTS US STILL. PROCLAIMED THE largest ship in the world, widely touted as unsinkable, she hit an iceberg on her maiden voyage and went down, taking with her many of the great celebrities of the day as well as hundreds of immigrants hoping for a fresh start in the New World.

The *Titanic* is enthralling because she was not just a ship; she was a symbol. Throughout the nineteenth century, people gradually developed a sense of security; by 1912 there had been nearly one hundred years of peace and a century of steady and astounding industrial progress. The *Titanic* burst that bubble.

Then, as now, the *Titanic* story appealed to people on many different levels: the romance of the great age of ocean travel; the fascination of the ultimate shipwreck; the enticement of endless trivia. Above all, the *Titanic* entrances me as a social historian. Her enduring allure surely has as much to do with the world she represented as with the dramatic story she has to tell. She provides an exquisite microcosm of the Edwardian world, illuminating its strict class distinctions, its obsession with etiquette and fashion, and, inevitably, its love of fine food.

In the course of my research for *A Night to Remember*, I got to know many *Titanic* survivors, including Mrs. Henry B. Harris, whose husband, a prominent Broadway theatrical producer, went down with the ship. When I knew René Harris in the early 1950s, she had long since lost her fortune in the stock market crash of 1929 and was reduced to a single room in a welfare hotel in New York City. But she had lost neither her sunny disposition nor her theatrical poise.

One day I brought her a little jar of caviar in an attempt to give this gallant lady a taste of the good old days. She sampled it once, then pushed the jar politely aside. "You call that caviar?" she asked with cheerful incredulity. She wasn't playing a role. Before the days of pasteurization and government health inspectors, caviar did taste different. And perhaps better.

Reproducing the *Titanic*'s marvelous food is surely one of the best ways to experience a bygone age of luxury and leisure. Thanks to the testimony of eyewitnesses and the survival of several actual menus—including the final dinner in both first and second class—what the *Titanic*'s passengers ate can be re-created to a remarkable degree of authenticity. Through the most revealing of social customs, the preparation and consumption of food, *Last Dinner on the Titanic* provides a wonderful window into the social life of an Edwardian age steaming unwittingly toward oblivion.

Every year on or near April 14, a surprisingly large number of sentimentalists sit down to a dinner based on the menus that survive from that final day. *Last Dinner on the Titanic* puts such a lively historical re-creation within reach of anyone who loves to cook, enabling an even wider audience to relive a great moment in history.

—Walter Lord,
author of *A Night to Remember*

"We dined the last night in the Ritz restaurant. It was the last word in luxury. The tables were gay with pink roses and white daisies, the women in their beautiful shimmering gowns of satin and silk, the men immaculate and well-groomed, the stringed orchestra playing music from Puccini and Tchaikowsky. The food was superb: caviar, lobster, quail from Egypt, plover's eggs, and hothouse grapes and fresh peaches. The night was cold and clear, the sea like glass."

— First-class passenger Mrs. Walter Douglas

Last Dinner *on the* Titanic

AN ESSAY

O N THE EVENING OF APRIL 14, 1912, FEW OF THE DINERS IN THE *TITANIC*'S À LA CARTE restaurant noticed that the vibrations of the ship's engines had noticeably increased over the last few hours. They were far too engaged in the rich repast unfolding before them like a series of acts in a well-rehearsed play. Those who did notice began to speculate that the increased speed meant an earlier than predicted arrival in New York—Tuesday night

rather than Wednesday morning—and mentally resolved to send their steward to the purser's office with a telegram for dispatch to the people who would be meeting them at the White Star pier.

Most of the first-class passengers basking in the prestige of the *Titanic*'s maiden voyage were wealthy Americans, returning home after the winter season on the Continent. They belonged to a transatlantic leisure class, a recently evolved breed that led what seemed, in the years before the First World War, a charmed life. *Titanic* chronicler Walter Lord has called them the cosmopolites, "a large set of fashionable people" whose lifestyle "went

far beyond the boundaries of any one nation. Americans, British, and a sprinkling of Continentals, they lived an international life of their own . . . restlessly migrating from country to country, from season to season. They were extravagant, frivolous, often foolish, but they were perhaps the most truly cosmopolitan group the world has ever seen."

Just a glance around the expensively appointed room, done up in the style of Louis Seize in an effort to mimic the lavishness of a five-star hotel, confirmed the wealth and status of the diners. Walter Douglas, multimillionaire director of Quaker Oats, and his wife sat at one of the smaller alcove

Once dressed for dinner, passengers could either walk down the forward grand staircase to the dining saloon on D-deck or take one of the ship's three first-class elevators, located near the staircase.

Dining in the à la carte restaurant on the evening of April 14, 1912, were J. Bruce Ismay (top), managing director of the White Star Line, fashion entrepreneur Lady Duff-Gordon (above), and popular writer Jacques Futrelle (right).

tables. At another table for two, J. Bruce Ismay, managing director of the White Star Line and the driving force behind the construction of the *Titanic* and her sister ship, *Olympic*, chatted amiably with Dr. W. F. N. O'Loughlin, the ship's doctor and one of White Star's longest serving and most popular employees. Nearby sat Sir Cosmo and Lady Duff-Gordon, traveling incognito under the names of Mr. and Mrs. Morgan. Lady Duff-Gordon, sister to the famed Elinor Glyn, owned and ran a fabulously successful fashion house known as Madame Lucile, with branches in London, Paris, and New York. Perhaps she and her husband had bought their tickets under assumed names to avoid attention—or perhaps a temporary cash flow crisis had forced Lucile to hide from some predatory creditor.

One of the liveliest tables was occupied by the Harrises and the Futrelles. Jacques Futrelle, a successful mystery writer, soon fell into animated discussion about the current crop of Broadway plays with René Harris, whose husband, Henry, was one of New York's top theater producers. While these and other notables examined their menus and sipped their aperitifs, smartly clad waiters moved skillfully among them, the stage managers of the culinary drama.

That evening the watchful eye of restaurant manager Luigi Gatti never strayed far from the large table where a lavish dinner party was being hosted by Mr. and Mrs. George Widener of Philadelphia. Widener ruled Philadelphia's street railway system, the powerful enterprise that had made his father the richest man in the city and bankrolled the family's country estate, whose palatial manor housed an art museum's worth of paintings. The Wideners' accumulated wealth permitted their unmarried twenty-seven-year-old son, Harry, who was traveling with them, to devote the bulk of his entrepreneurial energy to the acquisition of rare and antique books. The prize from his recent visit to London was a much-coveted edition of Francis Bacon's *Essays*, dated 1598, which Harry kept with him at all times.

Two other prominent Philadelphia couples joined the Wideners that evening—the Thayers and the Carters. Like George Widener, John B. Thayer had inherited most of his considerable wealth, but he had also worked his way from clerk to second vice president of the Pennsylvania Railroad. Although

One of the most famous dinner parties given on board ship was hosted by George Widener (top) and his wife Eleanor (above) in honor of Captain Edward J. Smith. Smith is seated at the head of the table (opposite) in a re-creation of luncheon in the first-class dining saloon for the 1958 movie *A Night to Remember.*

William E. Carter's income derived from his father's talent for acquiring coal mines, his social status had been enhanced by his marriage to Lucille Polk, descended from a relative of James Knox Polk, the eleventh president of the United States.

Joining these grandees of Philadelphia society were two of the *Titanic*'s most sought-after table companions, Captain Edward J. Smith, the ship's urbane and popular commanding officer, and Major Archibald Butt, President William Howard Taft's friend and military aide, the ship's most famous bachelor.

Eleanor Widener had chosen the menu in advance, after consultation with Signor Gatti and, most likely, with advice from Executive Chef Rousseau's personal secretary, Paul Maugé. But we can only surmise what these luminaries ate. Unlike the ship's three dining saloons, all operated by White Star employees and serving a fixed menu that changed daily, the à la carte restaurant was operated as an independent concession by a separate staff

Archibald Butt (above) looked every inch the dashing *aide-de-camp*, just as Captain Smith (right) presented the perfect image for a commodore of the White Star Line.

with its own kitchen. Gatti, who had cut his teeth at London's famed Ritz Hotel, had been hired away from the posh Oddenino's Imperial Restaurant of Piccadilly; he counted ten of his cousins among his staff. Like a hotel restaurant on land, this mid-ocean dining room offered a wide-ranging à la carte menu—hence its name—tuned to the rich palates and enormous appetites of the era. All we can safely assume is that the Wideners and their guests ate many courses in considerable quantities and that the food was fresh, prepared to the standard of the best hotel restaurants, and accompanied by excellent ports and expensive wines. No doubt the special menu Chef Rousseau had prepared included some of the delicacies remembered by the survivors who ate in the restaurant that night: caviar, lobster, perhaps in a rich cream sauce, and quails, roasted lightly in a hot oven, then possibly finished with a succulent sauce of brandy and fresh cherries.

In the rosy light of recollection, the food on the *Titanic* grew more splendid after the ship had sunk, but there seems no question that the meals were fabulous indeed. Many remarked that the fare in second class, which shared its galley with the first-class dining saloon, was as good or better than the best fare on most ocean liners of the day. However, the *Titanic* and the *Olympic* were not the first to boast a hotel-style restaurant for the pleasure of their wealthiest passengers. In fact, the reason many survivors from first class referred to the *Titanic's* restaurant as the "Ritz" was that they had previously dined in one of the ocean-going Ritz rooms aboard the finest ships of the Hamburg-Amerika Line. This German-owned enterprise had single-handedly raised the standard of shipboard cuisine in the previous few years, and it was with Hamburg-Amerika

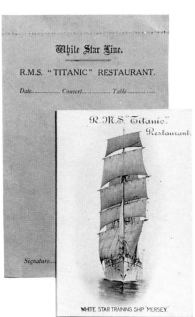

Two rare items from the *Titanic's* restaurant: a menu cover (front) and a waiter's order pad.

that White Star was obviously, and it now seemed successfully, competing.

It is tempting to speculate on the conversational gambits pursued by the Wideners and their guests as the appetizer yielded to the soup, the soup gave way to the fish, then entrées, sorbet, roasts, cold dishes, and finally the dessert. By the time the party repaired to the reception room for after-dinner coffee and, perhaps, a cordial (the term in those days for a strong drink after dinner), they had surely spent a good deal of time discussing the new ship and complimenting Captain Smith on the blaze of glory with which he was ending his distinguished career. The *Titanic's* maiden voyage was to be his last.

Who can doubt that the evening passed agreeably, with each successive sip of wine and bite of delicious food making the *Titanic* seem even more marvelous? Perhaps someone raised the rumor that the ship had entered iceberg territory, gossip that Smith would have unhesitatingly confirmed. In fact, he may well have told them, he had seen another iceberg warning just before dinner and the ship's crew was taking all the usual precautions—but there was no need at this point to slow the liner down.

"The men of my coterie would always go to the smoking room, and almost every evening join in conversation with some of the well-known men we met there...."

— First-class passenger Archibald Gracie

The *Titanic*'s smoking room was a strictly male preserve whose decor was intended to evoke the atmosphere of a private men's club. Among its amenities were specially designed White Star matchboxes (left).

The night was clear and the lookouts in the crow's nest would be able to spot a berg in ample time to alter course.

The captain lingered in the reception room long enough to smoke a second cigar. Ever the punctilious commander and dutiful White Star employee, he had consumed not a drop of alcohol during the course of the evening. Just before 9 P.M., he thanked his hosts and excused himself. Before turning in, Smith headed for the bridge to pay one last visit to the officers on duty. After a few minutes desultory conversation with his second officer, Charles Lightoller, in command of the watch until 10 P.M., he parted with these final words: "If it becomes at all doubtful let me know at once. I will be just inside." In all likelihood he was soon sleeping peacefully.

Meanwhile, the Widener dinner party dispersed. Archie Butt, young Harry Widener, and William Carter walked up one deck to the first-class smoking room for a cigar, a nightcap, and very likely some serious financial talk not suitable for mixed company. Those passengers who ventured onto the promenade deck for an after-dinner stroll were in for something of a shock. The air had become bitterly cold. Soon most of the passengers on board the R.M.S. *Titanic* had slipped snugly between crisp, clean sheets to be lulled toward slumber by the gentle thrum of the huge reciprocating engines far below.

By 11 P.M., the stewards and their assistants in the à la carte restaurant and in the ship's three dining saloons had finished clearing away dinner,

set up for breakfast, and returned to their quarters. The feverish activity in the galleys had slowed, most of the cooks having retired for a few hours of well-earned slumber while the scullions, glassmen, and plate washers neared the end of their exhausting and repetitive tasks. But for some the work was just beginning. Walter Belford, chief night baker, was already busy preparing rolls and fresh bread for the morning meal. Even as the fifth day of the *Titanic*'s maiden voyage drew to a close, the elaborate cycle of food preparation and service had begun again.

MORE THAN EIGHTEEN HOURS earlier, long before dawn, on what would prove to be the last day of the *Titanic*'s life, various crew members had begun to stir from their bunks in the big dormitories on E-deck. Soon the galley that served both the first- and second-class dining saloons was bustling with cooks preparing for the morning's breakfast, and sauciers beginning work on the elaborate gravies that would enrich the evening meal. When most of the rest of the *Titanic*'s sixty chefs and assistants plus their kitchen support staff of thirty-six reported for duty, all but the most insomniac passengers were still sleeping soundly. And few of the contented voyagers were yet out of bed when the stewards started work at six.

It took a huge staff to prepare the food for the *Titanic*'s 2,223 passengers and crew in the days before technology replaced so much manual labor.

Most of the non-navigational crew on board devoted all their time to the needs of the travelers in first and second class, who expected service on par with that of a five-star hotel. It seems safe to estimate that there were as many staff as passengers in first and second class and that the majority of these were involved in preparing or serving food. Besides the captain, the most important men on the ship were the chief engineer and the head chef. And the chef's pay, when gratuities were included, would have been second only to that of Captain Smith. Given the *Titanic*'s emphasis on luxury, especially when it came to food, this pecuniary hierarchy makes sense. Along with his culinary talents, Charles Proctor needed the organizational abilities of a commander-in-chief fighting a war on several fronts.

The planning and execution of each day's three main meals, plus assorted snacks and light meals, required extensive advance preparation and precise timing—not to mention huge quantities of raw material. As one of the first ocean liners to make fine food a priority—a fact reflected in the impressive scope of her provision list—the *Titanic* required unprecedented on-board storage facilities. These included separate refrigerators for each type of perishable—meat, fish, fruit, vegetables, eggs, and dairy products—and separate cold storage for vintage wines and spirits. From mundane supplies such as cereals (10,000 pounds) and sugar (5 tons) to more exotic items such as fresh asparagus (800 bundles) and oysters (1,221 quarts), the *Titanic*'s larder was full to overflowing with the best fresh food.

At 7 A.M., the earliest rising first-class passengers were served morning tea or coffee and fruit, and perhaps fresh-baked scones with jam or marmalade in their staterooms. Thus refreshed, they were up and dressed by the time the breakfast bugle sounded at 8 A.M. and their steward arrived with a personal copy of the *Atlantic Daily Bulletin*, the *Titanic*'s own daily newspaper.

The formality of upper-class Edwardians ensured that no one arrived in the splendid first-class dining saloon in bedroom slippers. In fact, most breakfasters would have been dressed for Sunday services—scheduled to be held in the dining saloons at 10:30 A.M.—the men in blue blazers, or light tweed or flannel suits with matching vests, the women in pale-colored light wool skirts, perhaps with matching jacket, and high-necked white blouses of fine lawn cotton. Probably some of the earliest rising ladies found time to change their clothes for church; the rest returned to their staterooms only for the addition of hats and gloves.

Couture seems to have been the reigning preoccupation of the wealthy women of this era. As Lady Cynthia Asquith later recalled, "It must be admitted that a very large fraction of our time was spent in dressing and undressing. We were for ever changing our clothes, a custom which necessitated traveling with a mountain of luggage—at least one large domed trunk called a Noah's Ark, an immense hat box and a heavy fitted dressing case." Many of the first-class ladies were attended by a personal maid and some of the gentlemen by a manservant. One also brought along his newly purchased Renault touring car, complete with chauffeur.

"It must be admitted that a very large fraction of our time was spent in dressing and undressing. We were for ever changing our clothes, a custom that necessitated traveling with a mountain of luggage."

— Lady Cynthia Asquith

The Edwardians did not travel lightly, as evidenced by the luggage waiting to be loaded on board the *Titanic*'s sister ship, *Olympic* (above). Many of the American women on the *Titanic* were bringing home the latest fashions from Paris.

The Morning Tea-tray

R.M.S "TITANIC"
APRIL 11, 1912

BAKED APPLES   FRESH FRUIT   STEWED PRUNES
QUAKER OATS   BOILED HOMINY   PUFFED RICE
FRESH HERRINGS
FINDON HADDOCK   SMOKED SALMON
GRILLED MUTTON KIDNEYS & BACON
GRILLED HAM   GRILLED SAUSAGE
LAMB COLLOPS   VEGETABLE STEW
FRIED, SHIRRED, POACHED & BOILED EGGS
PLAIN & TOMATO OMELETTES TO ORDER
SIRLOIN STEAK & MUTTON CHOPS TO ORDER
MASHED, SAUTE & JACKET POTATOES
COLD MEAT
VIENNA & GRAHAM ROLLS
SODA & SULTANA SCONES   CORN BREAD
BUCKWHEAT CAKES
BLACK CURRANT CONSERVE   NARBONNE HONEY
OXFORD MARMALADE
WATERCRESS

"The exercise and the swim gave me an appetite for a hearty breakfast. Then followed the church service in the dining saloon."

— First-class passenger
Archibald Gracie

Early risers could request that tea be served in their staterooms, an Edwardian indulgence idealized in this period illustration (left). A first-class breakfast menu from April 11 (above) shows the hearty bill of fare.

The Edwardian breakfast was indeed a feast fit for a king—as the surviving breakfast menus from the *Titanic* attest. It is doubtful, however, that anyone on board ate as much to start the day as had the recently deceased King Edward VII, whose enormous appetite set the tone for an age of excess. For the large-girthed Edward, breakfast meant a huge meal that began with haddock, followed by grilled meat

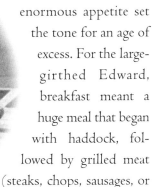

(steaks, chops, sausages, or cutlets), then poached eggs, all brought to a stomach-turning close by spit-roasted chickens and woodcock.

Breakfast in second class was hardly less sumptuous and even in steerage no one was complaining. Until not long before, third-class passengers had been expected to bring along enough food to sustain them through an Atlantic crossing. But few of the elite would have found the steerage fare to their liking, with its choice of oatmeal porridge, smoked herring, jacket potatoes, tripe and onions, and virtually inedible cabin biscuits.

At sea, however, it was not long since things had been little better in first class. Charles Dickens, after traveling to America on Cunard's *Britannia* in 1842, complained that the first-class dining room resembled a "gigantic hearse with

The Edwardians

Although King Edward VII died in 1910, the Edwardian era is commonly held to have ended with the outbreak of the First World War. Those years between the turn of the century and "the war to end all wars" were a transitional period, marking the shift from the official puritanism of the Victorian age to a less inhibited style epitomized by Edward himself. He was a big man with a warm personality who dressed well, kept a mistress, lived lavishly, and loved entertaining. It was Edward and his circle, for example, who broke the convention that forbade respectable women to dine in public. They regularly patronized the Savoy Hotel and later the London Ritz, when it opened in 1906. Edward was an apt symbol for a self-confident upper class that believed deeply in Progress and enjoyed tweaking convention, but never doubted its God-given right to wealth and privilege.

windows" and commented dryly that a "very yellow boiled leg of mutton" followed by "a rather moldy dessert of apples, grapes and oranges" represented the acme of shipboard cuisine in his day.

No such complaints are recorded from any of the *Titanic*'s survivors. We can imagine most of them gladly seeking the promenade deck or the boat deck to breathe some fresh air and walk off their considerable breakfasts before making a weekly peace with their God.

T HE FIRST- AND SECOND-CLASS dining saloon stewards barely had time between the end of Sabbath devotions and the 1 P.M. bugle to reset the dining saloons for Sunday luncheon. In first class, the religious service had been conducted by Captain Smith, who seemed to revel in such ceremonial functions; second class had to settle for the assistant purser, Reginald Barker. The second-class dining saloon, slightly smaller and somewhat less opulent than first class, was nonetheless a spacious and attractive room.

On the *Titanic*, second class meant "middle class," a solid social stratum characterized more by Victorian probity than Edwardian license in its devotion to God, work, country, and duty. Typical of this group was a young London schoolmaster named Lawrence Beesley, on his way to visit his brother in America.

Unfortunately, no one from second class reported much about the food—except that it

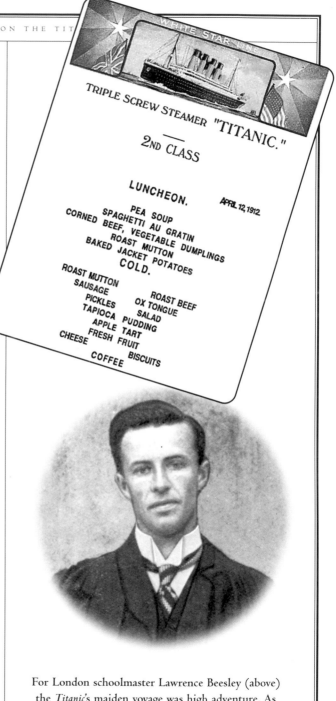

TRIPLE SCREW STEAMER "TITANIC."

2ND CLASS

LUNCHEON. APRIL 12, 1912

PEA SOUP
SPAGHETTI AU GRATIN
CORNED BEEF, VEGETABLE DUMPLINGS
ROAST MUTTON
BAKED JACKET POTATOES
COLD.
ROAST MUTTON
SAUSAGE ROAST BEEF
PICKLES OX TONGUE
TAPIOCA PUDDING SALAD
APPLE TART
FRESH FRUIT
CHEESE BISCUITS
COFFEE

For London schoolmaster Lawrence Beesley (above) the *Titanic*'s maiden voyage was high adventure. As indicated by the sample lunch menu (top), he and his fellow second-class passengers enjoyed a more generous luncheon than most would have known at home.

was good and plentiful and a great deal finer than what most were used to at home. But one second-class luncheon menu survives, so we have an idea of the sort of fare enjoyed by the young science teacher and his companions at Assistant Purser Barker's table. As the bright April sunlight streamed in the port-side portholes, they tucked into a hearty soup, then a hot roast, followed by an assortment of cold meats and salads, dessert, fresh fruit, and cheese.

As a science teacher, Beesley took great interest in the *Titanic* as technological marvel, an interest shared by at least two of his fellow diners: Douglas Norman, a Scottish engineer on his way to Vancouver, and Hilda Slayter, whose brother was a White Star captain.

Talk that day inevitably turned to the daily distance record, posted every noon outside the purser's office. In the previous twenty-four hours, the *Titanic* had traveled 546 miles, the greatest distance covered so far. And the massive ship had not yet fired up all

This White Star Line trading card promotes the *Titanic* and her almost identical sister, the *Olympic*, which had entered service in 1911. The *Olympic* would survive the First World War and remain a popular passenger liner until 1935.

of its boilers, so there was the prospect of an even more impressive twenty-four hour total to come. Yet the engine vibrations were as yet barely noticeable, and unlike the faster Atlantic liners, such as Cunard's *Mauretania* and *Lusitania*, which had an unpleasant "screw-like motion" when traveling at high speeds, the *Titanic* rose gently up and down as she rode the ocean swells. Miss Slayter, who had crossed the Atlantic many times, assured her table companions that the new White Star liner was the most commodious and comfortable ship on which she had ever sailed.

After lunch most passengers occupied themselves with intimate or solitary pursuits—writing letters or curling up with a book in the second-class library or in the first-class reading and writing room, playing a quiet game of cards, strolling alone or in small groups on deck, or lying (well wrapped up) in a deck chair while warming themselves with a cup of hot beef broth served by an attentive steward. A few more energetic souls visited the *Titanic*'s state-of-the-

*"There was a constant state
of war between the walkers,
usually vigorous early risers,
and the occupants of deck chairs
in their path, who had probably
been driven from their bunks
by the racket overhead."*

— John Maxtone-Graham in
The Only Way to Cross

art gymnasium. Those in search of less strenuous physical release took a Turkish sauna followed by a dip in the ship's swimming pool, or booked a massage with one of the Turkish bath attendants. First-class passengers in need of additional refreshment took coffee in the Verandah and Palm Court or afternoon tea in the Café Parisien, like the à la carte restaurant, a concession operated under the watchful eye of Luigi Gatti.

Unlike modern cruise ships, the *Titanic*'s staff included no professionally enthusiastic cruise director endlessly promoting organized group activities. But in the first five days of the voyage, new friendships had formed and old ones been renewed. And that lovely feeling of isolated containment, combined with the relaxation of one's sense of time that comes only with a long ocean voyage or train journey, meant that few passengers were restless or bored as the sunny afternoon slipped quietly away.

By the time the 6 P.M. bugle called the passengers to dress for dinner, the outside air temperature had dropped to an almost wintry cold, which provided an excuse to make Sunday dinner the most glittering meal of the voyage so far. As first-class passenger Elmer Taylor recalled, "a smooth sea, clear skies and low temperature outside gave women passengers an opportunity to get out their latest Parisian gowns, their most brilliant jewels, transformation (a hairdo of the time), facial treatments etc. It was a brilliant assembly—contentment and happiness prevailed." Taylor's recollection is echoed by May

Futrelle, who later wrote, "It was a buoyant, oh, such a jolly, crowd. It was a rare gathering of beautiful women and splendid men."

Never had more wealth and privilege been gathered on a single ship. Despite the fact that some of the richest and most prominent first-class passengers—including the Wideners and their well-heeled dinner party—had elected to eat in the à la carte restaurant, the first-class saloon boasted an even more impressive list. At the top of the hierarchy mandated by money and status stood Colonel John Jacob Astor, one of the richest men in America, if not the world. Having divorced his first wife and—to Society's horror—married a woman younger than his son, he had fled to Europe with his bride to evade the publicity hounds and wait for the tide of public opinion to turn in his favor.

The slightly lower rungs were crowded with the merely wealthy—Benjamin Guggenheim, whose family's financial empire was intimately intertwined with that of J. Pierpont Morgan, ruler of a vast financial conglomerate that included the White Star Line itself; steel magnate Arthur Ryerson; Isidor Straus, co-founder of Macy's department store; Charles M. Hays, president of the Canadian Grand Trunk Railroad; and Washington Roebling, whose uncle's engineering firm had supervised the construction of the Brooklyn Bridge. Likely the most raucous first-class table that evening was presided over by Mrs. James J. Brown, estranged wife of a Denver gold-mining tycoon who now made Newport

"There was not the slightest thought of danger in the minds of those who sat around the tables in the luxurious dining saloon of the Titanic. It was a brilliant crowd. Jewels flashed from the gowns of the women. And, oh, the dear women, how fondly they wore their latest Parisian gowns! It was the first time that most of them had an opportunity to display their newly acquired finery."

— First-class passenger
Mrs. Jacques Futrelle

her home base. Loud, coarse-tongued, and ever ready to regale an audience with wild stories of her many adventures, Molly Brown made sure she was unforgettable—even before the events that would earn her the sobriquet "unsinkable." The mood throughout first class that night was festive. As one passenger recalled, "Everybody was so merry. We were all filled with the joy of living. We sat over dinner late that night."

And what a dinner it was, the finest of the voyage so far. Chef Proctor and his legions had outdone themselves with an eleven-course feast that would leave most modern diners gasping for air. The meal began with a choice of raw oysters or hors d'oeuvre variés, which was followed by either consommé Olga or cream of barley soup. True to Edwardian fashion, greatly influenced by the elaborate and heavily sauced cuisine perfected by the French master Auguste Escoffier, many of the main dishes were made richer and more delicious with high-fat sauces and garnishes.

One of the more fascinating entries on the menu card was *Punch Romaine*. More like an

John Jacob Astor (above) was the richest man on board. Benjamin Guggenheim (below) was traveling with his young French mistress, a "Madame" Aubart, who took all her meals in the à la carte restaurant.

alcoholic sorbet than any punch consumed today, this Escoffier concoction would have been served in dessert cups as a palate cleanser between the fifth course (the remove)—a choice of lamb, roast duckling, or sirloin of beef —and the seventh (the roast)— on this occasion a roasted squab accompanied by fresh watercress.

After dinner, many in first class visited the reception room next door, where they drank small cups of strong coffee while listening to the *Titanic*'s orchestra play a concert of light classics and popular favorites that closed with tunes from Offenbach's perennially popular *The Tales of Hoffman*. In second class, Lawrence Beesley and his shipboard acquaintance, Reverend Ernest Carter, had arranged a hymn-sing in the dining saloon. In third class, an impromptu party that had been going since 3 P.M. ended sharply at 10 when the stewards turned out the lights.

Soon after 11 P.M., when the stewards closed down the first- and second-class lounges, the ship grew quiet, except for the two smoking rooms, where serious card playing and drinking continued as midnight approached. Among these

"Some said it was poor on its Wagner work; others said the violin was weak. But that was for conversation's sake, for nothing on board was more popular than the orchestra."

— First-class passenger Helen Churchill Candee

Seven of the eight musicians on board the *Titanic*, including their leader, violinist Wallace Hartley, who is pictured in the center. The players usually worked in two separate string ensembles, a quintet in the reception room of the first-class dining saloon and a trio in the lounge outside the à la carte restaurant. They would accommodate almost any request, even if it wasn't listed in the White Star music book (right).

late revelers were Archie Butt, Harry Widener, and William Carter, who had repaired to these congenial quarters when the Wideners' dinner party broke up.

At precisely 11:40 P.M., the ship gave a shudder almost unnoticeable to most. In the first-class galley, Chief Night Baker Walter Belford felt the slight swaying motion that was enough to send a pan of freshly baked rolls clattering to the floor. The men in the second-class smoking room had actually observed an iceberg pass by, but were so engrossed in their card games that no one even ventured out on deck to see if anything was the matter. Only when the *Titanic*'s powerful engines grew unnaturally still did any of the ship's more privileged passengers, all of them situated far away from the point of the hull's slight but fatal impact, even guess that anything might be wrong—a dropped propeller blade, perhaps, or a nearby ship in distress. Only the stokers far below in the breached forward boiler rooms knew beyond doubt that R.M.S. *Titanic*'s maiden voyage had come to an end.

WHITE STAR LINE

MUSIC

Choreographing *a* First-Class Titanic Dinner

THERE IS MORE TO RE-CREATING THE FINAL FIRST-CLASS dinner on the *Titanic* than cooking and serving the dishes we describe in this book. Just as important is the sense of expectation that precedes the event and the sense of occasion as the dinner unfolds.

Many weeks before the day, send out handwritten, formal invitations. Once your guests have accepted, send them an envelope of information, including advice on what to wear (evening clothes for the men, close-fitting, floor-length gowns for the women) and perhaps a biography of the character each is being asked to play. If you want to really get into the spirit of things, you could provide facsimiles of actual cabin tickets, filled out with their names, the number of servants accompanying them, and the number of cubic feet of luggage to be taken.

Set your table elaborately—decorate it with fresh flowers and bowls of fruit, place a folded White Star Line menu card at each place and a red

*"Inside this floating palace that spring evening
in 1912, warmth and lights, the hum of voices,
the gay lilt of a German waltz — the unheeding
sounds of a small world bent on pleasure."*

— First-class passenger Lady Duff-Gordon

carnation boutonniere for each of the gentlemen. Accompany the meal with the gentle strains of the Palm Court music popular at the time. The more you can choreograph the evening to create a period atmosphere, the more you and your guests will feel as though you've traveled back in time to the evening of April 14, 1912.

Before Dinner

In the "reception room," (the most elegant room in your house, apart from the dining room), the host introduces each gentleman to the lady he will "take down" to dinner and with whom he will converse while drinks are served. In 1912, cocktails were the rage, and many people enjoyed a mixed drink as an aperitif—a habit frowned on by French gastronomes. However, since the evening contains a good deal of alcohol, you may prefer to start your guests off with something lighter, a glass of white wine, perhaps, or some champagne. If you want to begin the food before the assembly is called to table, serve the hors d'oeuvre in the reception room.

During Dinner

On the *Titanic*, a bugler called the passengers to dinner with the tune "The Roast Beef of Old England." Unless there's a trumpet player in your immediate circle, announce dinner with the ringing of a gong. Each gentleman offers his right arm to his lady and escorts her to her place, which is always to his right, holds her chair for her, then sits down

himself. During the meal, his first responsibility is to engage her in conversation, but he may speak to the lady on his left if his dinner partner is occupied in conversation elsewhere.

If you are serving the dinner as it would have been served on board the ship, each course should be presented on a silver salver and passed around from guest to guest. If you have staff, then the steward offers each dish (always from the left) to each guest. In a meal of many courses, this has the advantage of permitting the diner to eat as little of each course as he or she wishes. Though the Edwardians had legendary appetites, no doubt some of those at dinner—particularly the younger ladies—would have politely demurred at certain courses, or taken only the smallest of portions.

As for the service of wine, you can make this as simple or as complex as you wish. At minimum, your guests should have separate glasses for red wine, white wine, and sparkling wine. To be absolutely correct, there should be a fresh glass with each new wine. Edwardians liked to drink, and the *Titanic* had a wide selection of excellent wines and champagnes, as well as spirits, brandies, and liqueurs. One writer claims the ship carried seventy brands of champagne, fifty-four types of Bordeaux, and forty-eight Burgundies, Moselles, and Italian wines. But so far, no actual wine list from the ship has come to light.

On the two first-class menus (see pages 47 and 67), we've provided generic suggestions for what type of wine would have been drunk with each course. These suggestions are based on the prevailing

The orchestra on another liner of the period (above) approximates the look of Wallace Hartley's ensemble. By the 1920s, a small orchestra provided music for dancing on the *Titanic*'s sister ship, *Olympic* (overleaf).

practice of the time and the fact that French wines would most certainly have predominated. You will want to narrow your wine selection depending on the dishes you actually serve.

Music

On the *Titanic* there were two musical ensembles— a five-piece orchestra under the baton of Wallace Hartley and a string trio. As passengers gathered in the reception room before the doors to the first-class dining saloon opened for dinner, the quintet serenaded them with light music while they sipped their before-dinner drinks. Once dinner began, Hartley's group presumably moved to the dining saloon and played appropriate background selections. After dinner, these same musicians could be found back in the reception room, where passengers remembered a delightful concert that closed with selections from Offenbach's *The Tales of Hoffman*.

The trio, which consisted of cello, violin and piano, played in the reception room adjoining the à la carte restaurant and the Café Parisien. The cellist was French and the violinist Belgian, adding to the overall Gallic flavor. Undoubtedly, the trio was

A Titanic Discography *and* Musical Bibliography

COMPACT DISCS

British Light Music. Archibald Joyce. Dublin RTE Orchestra. Andrew Penny, conductor. Marco Polo 8.223694. Among the many Joyce compositions of the period on this disc is "Songe d'Automne."

Titanic: Music as Heard on the Fateful Voyage. Ian Whitcomb conducting the White Star Orchestra. Rhino R2 72821. A wonderful compendium of authentic music played on authentic instruments.

Music Aboard the Titanic. Produced and arranged by Carl Wolfe. Inside Sounds Classic ISC-2896.

BOOKS

Turner, Michael R. and Antony Miall. *The Edwardian Song Book; Drawing-Room Ballads, 1900-1914, from the catalogue of Boosey & Co.* London: Methuen, 1982.

still playing when the Widener dinner party and their guest of honor, Captain Smith, took their after-dinner coffee.

If we don't know the precise programs these two sets of musicians played on the final evening, we do have a very good idea of their repertoire from the surviving White Star Line music book. It ran the gamut from grand opera (mostly French and Italian, though Wagner's *Tannhäuser* makes an appearance), light or comic opera (*The Mikado* by Sir Arthur Sullivan) to more popular song tunes and waltzes emanating from British music halls and musical comedies. And the musicians clearly were familiar with the jazzier rhythms of American ragtime, which had recently made its way across the Atlantic. While the ship was sinking, the band at one point played Irving Berlin's "Alexander's Ragtime Band."

One of the most popular contemporary British composers, Archibald Joyce, is represented by several entries in the music book. And, thanks to Walter Lord's research, we now know that a Joyce composition, a waltz called "Songe d'Automne," was almost certainly the last tune played before the *Titanic* sank.

Given the Edwardian love of ballad singing and the certainty that most of the ladies and many of the men would have been proficient pianists and able vocalists, it seems safe to assume that some diners would have participated in some after-dinner music-making of their own.

After Dinner

Following dessert, most passengers returned to the reception room for coffee, cordials, or port, and a concert of light classical music. Many of the men, Captain Smith included, smoked cigars. If there's a piano in the house and a pianist in the company, sheet music for Edwardian melodies is not hard to find.

Alternatively, you can follow the common Victorian and Edwardian custom of dividing the gentlemen and the ladies, the former repairing to a room or porch you've designated as the smoking room for cigars and port, the latter to your reception room for coffee.

At the end of the evening, bring everyone together in the reception room for final conversation and farewells.

The "Ritz" Restaurant

A period illustration (above) of diners in the *Olympic*'s à la carte restaurant, which was virtually identical to the *Titanic*'s, is framed in paneling from the actual room. A menu (left) from the *Olympic*'s restaurant.

R.M.S. *Olympic* Restaurant.

IF THE *TITANIC* WAS THE latest word in ocean-going luxury, then the "Ritz" restaurant was its most luxurious chamber, where the super-rich dined tête-à-tête on delicacies more rare than even the first-class dining saloon could provide. Everything about the room was designed to evoke the continental elegance of the finest hotel dining rooms in London or Paris: the light, French walnut paneling and furniture, the Louis Seize design and delicate Rose du Barri hue of the deep-pile Axminster carpet.

The à la carte restaurant imitated the fashionable and extremely popular Ritz-Carlton restaurants that graced the latest ships of the Hamburg-Amerika Line, where Auguste Escoffier had set the culinary standard and the staff were trained by César Ritz himself. Many passengers referred to the *Titanic*'s restaurant

The restaurant's Louis Seize decor (above) is echoed in the china pattern created expressly for the room by Royal Crown Derby. This plate (below) is a souvenir taken from the *Titanic* before she sailed.

as the "Ritz" because its service was similar to that offered by White Star's German rivals. The restaurant stayed open from 8 A.M. to 11 P.M. and the menu changed daily to cater to every aristocratic whim. Those passengers who took and paid for all their meals here, instead of in the first-class dining saloon, could apply for a rebate at the end of the voyage. After the sinking, several survivors did just that, confirming that the restaurant had become an immediate hit. So successful was the restaurant on the *Titanic*'s sister ship, *Olympic*, that it was soon expanded to accomodate the increased demand.

"*The restaurant, situated on the bridge deck, will be considered by many competent judges the most enticing apartment in the vessel.*"

— *The Shipbuilder*, 1911

A period painting (above) suggests the style of the diners in the *Titanic*'s restaurant. The *Olympic*'s restaurant (right) was a virtually identical room.

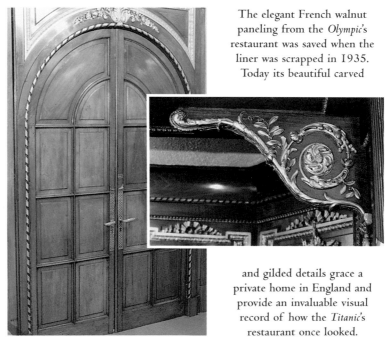

The elegant French walnut paneling from the *Olympic*'s restaurant was saved when the liner was scrapped in 1935. Today its beautiful carved and gilded details grace a private home in England and provide an invaluable visual record of how the *Titanic*'s restaurant once looked.

WHITE STAR LINE.

R.M.S. "OLYMPIC" (Triple Screw), 46,358 Tons.

THE LARGEST STEAMER IN THE WORLD.

LOUIS XVI. À LA CARTE RESTAURANT.

WHITE STAR LINE.

WINE, &c. ORDER.

Article _____

Date _____

_____ Passenger.

This cover from a 1911 brochure for the *Olympic* (above) demonstrates the importance White Star accorded the à la carte restaurant as a feature of their liner. The order card (left) was used to keep track of beverage requests in the restaurant.

R. M. S. "Olympic"
Restaurant.

.:. *Souper.* .:.

Paillettes au Parmesan
Amandes Salées   Olives

Consommé Gettysburg

Filets de Sole Florida

Délice de Pauillac aux Petits Pois
Pommes Nouvelles au Beurre

Pâté de Foie Gras en Croûte

— BUFFET FROID —
Jambon d'York   Galantine de Volaille
Langue Epicurienne   Poulet
Salade de Saison

Macédoine de Fruits Independence
Bonheur des Dames

This *Olympic* restaurant menu (above) designed for a July 4, 1914 celebration supper, offers a suggestion of the kind of fare that would have been served in the *Titanic*'s restaurant. Diners who took all their meals in the à la carte restaurant were entitled to a modest reimbursement, which was recorded on a receipt ticket (opposite). (Below) A White Star water carafe.

THE MENU FROM THE À LA CARTE restaurant must have been extensive and likely favored complex dishes that could show off the talents of Chef Rousseau. Unfortunately, none of the surviving passengers who ate there on the last evening tucked a copy of the menu into the pocket of a dinner jacket, so we can only surmise what the bill of fare included. Undoubtedly, the diners in the "Ritz" could enjoy a meal at least as opulent as that offered in the first-class dining saloon.

But many diners would have selected a reduced number of courses according to their appetites and palates. The menu we present here is one we have invented based on the fragments of evidence describing what was actually eaten that night — caviar, lobster, and "plover eggs" (we've substituted quail eggs). This menu comprises a series of courses, following the classic pattern, that a knowledgeable diner might have chosen from a similar à la carte menu of the time. In all there are eight courses. A dessert of cheese and fruit makes an optional, but virtually obligatory, ninth course.

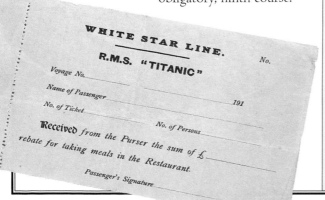

The Restaurant

FIRST COURSE — HORS D'OEUVRE
Oeufs de caille en aspic et caviar
White Bordeaux or White Burgundy

SECOND COURSE — POTAGE
Potage Saint-Germain
Madeira or Sherry

THIRD COURSE — POISSON
Homard Thermidor
Dry Rhine or Moselle

FOURTH COURSE — ENTRÉE
Tournedos aux morilles
Red Bordeaux

FIFTH COURSE — PUNCH OR SORBET
Punch Rosé

SIXTH COURSE — RÔTI
Cailles aux cerises
Red Burgundy

SEVENTH COURSE — LÉGUME
Asperges printanières, sauce hollandaise

EIGHTH COURSE — ENTREMETS
Macédoine de fruits
Oranges en surprise
Sweet Dessert Wines (Muscatel, Tokay, Madeira)

NINTH COURSE — LES DESSERTS
Assorted fresh fruits and cheeses
Sweet Dessert Wines, Champagne, or Sparkling Wine

AFTER DINNER
Coffee, cigars
Port or Cordials

Oeufs de caille en aspic et caviar
(Quail Eggs in Aspic with Caviar)

One of the diners in the Titanic's à la carte restaurant that last night recalled eating plover eggs with caviar.
Here we have substituted the more easily obtainable quail eggs. By 1912, the original use of aspic—to keep foods fresh and
appetizing looking—had been rendered obsolete by the advent of refrigeration. Instead, aspic provided an opportunity
for chefs to prepare dazzling visual creations.

9	small quail eggs
1/4 tsp	salt
2 cups	chilled consommé (see recipe page 73)
1 1/2 to 3 tsp	powdered gelatin
1/4	sweet red pepper
12	slices English cucumber
	Fresh flat-leaf (Italian) parsley
2 tbsp	sturgeon roe (caviar)
6	warm toast points

In pot, bring quail eggs covered with water to boil; cover and remove from heat. Let stand for 10 minutes; drain and run under cold water. Carefully peel eggs and pat dry; place in refrigerator to cool completely.

🍃 Stir salt into consommé; place 1 tbsp of consommé on chilled plate. Place in refrigerator for about 5 minutes. If well set, do not add any gelatin; however, if consommé is only lightly set, soften 1 1/2 tsp gelatin in 1/2 cup chilled consommé for 1 minute, then stir into remainder. (Likewise, if consommé is almost set, use only 1 tsp gelatin; or, if barely set, use up to 3 tsp gelatin.) Chill until thick but not set, about 20 minutes.

Meanwhile, cut red pepper into 2 equal pieces. Cut 1 piece of red pepper and cucumber slices into long, thin petal shapes. Using an aspic cutter or sharp knife, cut remaining red pepper into 6 small circles; pat dry and place in refrigerator until well chilled.

Pour 2 tbsp of the aspic into each of 6 parchment- or waxed-paper-lined ¹/₂-cup ramekins; tilt to cover surface evenly. Slice eggs in half lengthwise. Arrange 3 egg halves in bottom of each ramekin, yolk side up with narrow ends toward center so that eggs resemble flower petals. Arrange prepared vegetables and parsley leaves around eggs to make decorative flower designs (keep all decorations ¹/₈ inch away from edge of ramekin). Place in refrigerator for 15 minutes or until eggs and vegetables are set into jelly. Carefully spoon equal amounts of remaining aspic over top of each arrangement.

Place in refrigerator for 2 to 4 hours, or up to 24 hours, or until completely set. To serve, dip each ramekin into hot water for 5 seconds; invert onto serving plate and top with 1 tsp of caviar. Garnish with toast points. Makes 6 servings.

Tip: Do not use tinned or powdered consommé for this recipe, as it will not set properly.

SECOND COURSE — POTAGE

Potage Saint-Germain
(Spring Pea Soup)

*Named after the Comte de Saint-Germain, war minister to Louis XV,
this light soup is made from a puree of fresh green peas.*

1 tbsp	butter
¹/₂ cup	sliced leek, white part only
¹/₄ tsp	each salt and pepper
Pinch	granulated sugar
2 cups	shelled fresh or frozen tiny peas
1 cup	shredded romaine lettuce
2 tbsp	chopped fresh chervil or parsley
6 cups	chicken or vegetable stock
	Fresh chervil or parsley sprigs

In large saucepan, melt butter over medium heat; add leeks, salt, pepper, and sugar. Cook, stirring, for 5 minutes or until softened. Add peas, lettuce, chervil, and 1 cup of the stock; cover and cook over medium heat for 5 minutes or until peas are tender.

Working in batches and adding remaining stock, puree soup in blender or food processor; blend until very smooth. Strain through fine sieve and adjust seasoning if necessary.

Return to pan and reheat until steaming; skim off any foam. Ladle into serving bowls; garnish with a sprig of chervil or parsley. Makes 4 to 6 servings.

Homard Thermidor
(Lobster Thermidor with Duchess Potatoes)

This spectacular dish was created by the chef at Mairie's, one of the most famous restaurants of the Parisian Belle Époque, on the evening of January 19, 1894, in honor of the premiere of the play Thermidor *by Victorien Sardou. In an Edwardian restaurant, lobster thermidor was most often presented on a silver serving platter surrounded by a decorative (and delicious) border of duchess potatoes. Before serving, the entire plate was flashed under a broiler so that the topping on both lobster and potatoes would be golden brown and piping hot when the gloved waiter offered them at tableside.*

2	live Atlantic lobsters (2 lb each)
1/4 cup	butter, melted
2	cloves garlic, minced
1/2 cup	fresh bread crumbs
2 tbsp	finely chopped fresh chervil or parsley
1/4 tsp	each salt and pepper
	Duchess Potatoes (recipe follows)

SAUCE

1 cup	milk
1/2	onion, chopped
1	bay leaf
1/4 tsp	black peppercorns
2 tbsp	butter
2 tbsp	all-purpose flour
1 tsp	finely grated lemon zest
1 tsp	dry mustard
1/2 tsp	grated nutmeg
1/4 cup	whipping cream
1/4 tsp	each salt and white pepper

SAUCE: In small pot, heat milk, onion, bay leaf, and peppercorns over medium-high heat, just until bubbles begin to form around edges. Remove from heat; cover and let stand for 10 minutes.

In heavy saucepan, melt butter over medium heat; sprinkle over flour and cook for about 1 minute. Remove from heat and, whisking constantly, strain in hot milk. Return to medium heat and cook, whisking constantly, for 5 minutes or until sauce thickens enough to heavily coat back of spoon.

Stir in lemon zest, dry mustard, and nutmeg. Still stirring, gradually pour in whipping cream. Stir in salt and pepper. Cover and keep warm.

Cut lobsters in half lengthwise and remove claws; discard intestine, stomach, and gills. Pat dry; brush with enough melted butter to coat lightly. Sprinkle with salt and pepper and lay, shell side down, on baking sheet together with claws. Broil for 5 to 8 minutes or until shells are red and flesh is almost opaque. Cool slightly and remove flesh from tails; slice on angle. Crack claws and remove flesh; chop coarsely.

Coat inside of body shells with half of the reserved sauce. Arrange chopped lobster meat over sauce in shells. Coat evenly with remaining sauce and arrange on ovenproof serving platter.

In small bowl, stir together remaining butter, garlic, bread crumbs, chervil, salt, and pepper. Sprinkle evenly over lobsters. Place in 500°F oven for 5 minutes or until heated through. Add a border of Duchess Potatoes. Makes 4 servings.

"I had seen the cooks before their great cauldrons of porcelain, and the bakers turning out the huge loaves of bread, a hamper of which was later brought on deck, to supply the lifeboats."

— First-class passenger Marie G. Young

Duchess Potatoes

3	large baking potatoes, peeled and cut into chunks
1/4 cup	butter
1/4 tsp	each salt, pepper, nutmeg
1	egg
2	egg yolks
1 tbsp	butter, melted

In large pot of boiling salted water, cook potatoes until fork-tender. Drain well and turn out onto rimmed baking sheet. Place in 350°F oven for 2 minutes or until tray is dry.

❧ Transfer potatoes to large bowl and mash. Using electric mixer, whip butter, salt, pepper, and nutmeg into mashed potatoes. With beaters running, add egg and beat until thoroughly combined. Still beating, add yolks one at a time.

❧ Transfer potato mixture to piping bag fitted with star tube. Pipe decorative border around lobster on serving platter. Brush with melted butter and place under broiler for 1 minute or until lightly browned. Makes 2 cups.

Tip: Alternatively, larger portions of potato can be piped onto a serving tray in the shape of nests and baked at 375°F for 5 minutes or until lightly browned, then transferred, using a spatula, to individual serving plates.

Tournedos aux morilles
(Tournedos with Morels on a Bed of Braised Cabbage)

Nothing could be more elegant than this main dish of tender beef and wild mushrooms. Although it can be made with any type of mushroom, morels, which are among the most coveted of fungi, seem perfect for the à la carte restaurant at its finest hour. Traditionally the tournedos (also known as medallions or filets of beef) would have been served on a croûte, a potato cake, or a bed of braised cabbage to absorb the meat juices.

1/2 cup	dried morels
4	tournedos (6 oz each)
1/2 tsp	each salt and pepper
1 tbsp	vegetable oil
2 tbsp	butter
2 tbsp	chopped fresh parsley
	Braised Savoy Cabbage (recipe follows)

SAUCE

1/4 cup	butter
1/2	onion, finely chopped
1 1/2 cups	red wine
1/2 cup	port
1 cup	beef stock
	Salt and pepper

BRAISED SAVOY CABBAGE

3 oz	side bacon
1	onion, thinly sliced
1	medium Savoy cabbage, shredded
1/2 cup	chicken stock or water
1 tsp	granulated sugar
1 tbsp	white wine vinegar
1 tsp	chopped fresh thyme (or 1/2 tsp dried)
1/2 tsp	salt
1/4 tsp	pepper

Soak mushrooms in enough boiling water to cover for 15 to 20 minutes. Drain, reserving 1/2 cup soaking liquid.

❧ SAUCE: In saucepan, heat 1 tbsp of the butter over medium heat. Stir in onion and cook, stirring often, for 2 minutes; stir in red wine and port. Boil for 15 minutes or until reduced to about 1 cup. Add beef stock and reserved mushroom liquid. Continue to boil for 20 to 25 minutes or until reduced to about 1/2 cup. Strain into saucepan set over low heat; whisk in remaining butter, bit by bit. Season to taste. Keep warm.

❧ Meanwhile, season tournedos with salt and pepper. In skillet, heat oil and 1 tbsp of the butter over medium-high heat. Add meat and cook, turning once, for 8 to 10 minutes or until meat is well browned but still evenly pink inside. Remove to heated platter; increase heat to high and add remaining butter and mushrooms to same pan. Cook, stirring, for 2 to 3 minutes or until heated through and browned. Sprinkle with parsley and add to sauce.

❧ Serve tournedos on bed of braised Savoy cabbage. Ladle sauce around plate. Makes 4 servings.

Braised Savoy Cabbage
❧ Cut bacon into lardons (1 inch long by 1/4 inch thick). In large skillet, cook over medium-high heat for 5 minutes or until crisp and brown. Pour off all but 1 tbsp fat. Stir in onion, cabbage, stock, sugar, vinegar, thyme, salt, and pepper; cover and cook, stirring occasionally, for 10 to 12 minutes or until cabbage is tender but not mushy. Makes 4 servings.

Punch Rosé
(Rose Water and Mint Sorbet)

Although you can make your own rose water with organically grown rose petals, it can be found ready-made in a Middle Eastern market because it is still widely used in Middle Eastern and North African cooking. Rose water became popular in the seventeenth century as a flavoring for desserts and would have been familiar to Edwardian palates.

1 ¹/₂ cups	rose water
1 cup	water
¹/₂ cup	Simple Syrup (recipe follows)
¹/₄ cup	lightly packed mint leaves
1 ¹/₂ tsp	lemon juice
	SIMPLE SYRUP
2 cups	granulated sugar
1 cup	water

In blender or food processor, mix together rose water, water, simple syrup, mint leaves, and lemon juice. Blend until mint is finely chopped.

Pour into ice-cream maker and freeze following manufacturer's instructions. Or, pour mixture into chilled, shallow metal pan; cover and freeze for 2 hours or until firm. Break up into pieces and transfer to food processor; puree until smooth. Pour into chilled, airtight container; freeze for 20 minutes or until almost firm. Soften in refrigerator for 10 minutes before serving. Serve in chilled open champagne glasses or make ice bowls. Makes 2 ¹/₂ cups and serves 4 to 6.

Simple Syrup

In large pot, combine sugar and water; cook over medium heat, stirring gently, until sugar is completely dissolved. Bring to boil and cook for 1 minute or until syrup is clear. Let cool. (Syrup can be stored in a sterilized container in the refrigerator for up to one month.) Makes 2 cups.

Ice Bowls

Fill a small, shallow dish with enough water so that when another bowl is placed inside it, the water rises just to the rim of the outside dish. Freeze for 1 hour or until solid. Remove inside dish (use a small amount of hot water if necessary); decoratively place rose petals and mint leaves on top of ice. Freeze for 10 minutes or until decorations are secured to ice; pour in a few tablespoons of water to cover leaves and petals; freeze until needed.

Cailles aux cerises
(Quails with Cherries)

*Game birds were Edwardian favorites. In aristocratic
households, they could appear at any meal, even
breakfast, but their most bravura turn was as part of
a roast course, the soul of a classic French meal.*

4	jumbo quails (¹/₂ lb each)
1 tbsp	butter, softened
¹/₄ tsp	each salt and pepper
¹/₂ cup	port
¹/₂ cup	orange juice
2 tbsp	each cherry juice and brandy
¹/₂ cup	macerated, pitted cherries, drained and halved
1 tsp	chopped fresh tarragon
	Salad greens

Rinse and pat quails dry inside and out. Using kitchen scissors, remove wing tips. Stir together butter, salt, and pepper. Rub evenly over birds, inside and out; truss and place in ovenproof skillet. Cook over medium-high heat, turning often, for 5 minutes or until well browned on every side.

Remove quails from pan; add port, orange juice, cherry juice, and brandy. Bring to boil and cook for 3 to 5 minutes or until reduced by half; stir in cherries. Return quails to pan and cook, turning to coat, for 5 minutes or until nicely glazed. Place pan in 375°F oven for 10 minutes or until juices run pink. Stir in tarragon.

Cut away string. Serve quails with cherries and glaze drizzled over top; garnish each plate with salad greens. Makes 4 servings.

*Tip: Macerated cherries are cherries that have been soaked in sugar
and brandy overnight.*

Asperges printanières, sauce hollandaise
(Spring Asparagus Hollandaise)

In the Titanic's kitchens this delicious spring vegetable was likely cooked much longer than we would today, its soft texture blending with the silken richness of the hollandaise.

2 lb	asparagus
2	hard-cooked eggs, finely chopped
3 tbsp	finely chopped fresh parsley
	HOLLANDAISE
3/4 cup	unsalted butter
3 tbsp	water
3	egg yolks
1/4 tsp	each salt and white pepper
1 tbsp	lemon juice

HOLLANDAISE: In small saucepan or microwave-proof dish, melt butter; using spoon, skim froth from surface and discard. Cool slightly.

🌸 In top of double boiler or heatproof bowl, whisk water and egg yolks together with salt and pepper for 30 seconds or until pale yellow and frothy. Over barely simmering water, whisk mixture for 3 minutes or until it draws a ribbon for 5 seconds.

🌸 Remove pan from heat; whisk in warm butter, 1 tbsp at a time, until sauce begins to thicken. Still whisking, pour remaining butter into sauce in a slow, steady stream. Stir in lemon juice and adjust seasoning to taste. Keep warm by setting over a pot of warm water.

🌸 Holding asparagus halfway up stalk, snap off woody ends at natural breaking point and discard. In wide, deep skillet or large pot of boiling salted water, cook asparagus for 3 to 5 minutes or until tender. Drain well.

🌸 Arrange asparagus on shallow serving platter; pour sauce across center of stalks, leaving ends showing. Carefully sprinkle half of egg in a straight band across sauce. Next to this, sprinkle parsley; sprinkle remaining egg on other side of parsley. Makes 4 to 6 servings.

The trip couldn't help but be fun, and all the more if you were young and attractive like Gretchen Longley of Hudson, New York, a pretty American student in Paris. In her little cabin, she excitedly tore open a final bon voyage letter. It came from a friend left behind, who sent her a separate good wish for each day of the voyage:

Good Weather
Refreshments (Chocolate cake)
Every desire
Tommies to burn
Chocolate ice cream
Heavenly evenings
Entire meals
No regrets

— Walter Lord in *The Good Years*

No Edwardian meal was complete without a selection of sweets. Both of the recipes suggested here involve fresh fruit; its presence in early April meant that it had been transported a great distance from exotic climes such as southern Spain and North Africa.

Macédoine de fruits
(Fresh Fruit Salad)

This light, sweet dish is named for the ancient kingdom of Macedonia, birthplace of Alexander the Great.
It can be made from whatever combination of fresh fruit is on hand.

2	each pears, peaches and plums
1/2 cup	red currants or small raspberries
2 tbsp	lemon juice
3/4 cup	Simple Syrup (see page 53)
1/4 cup	lightly packed mint leaves
2 tbsp	kirsch or rum
1/4 cup	slivered almonds

Peel pears, peaches, and plums; dice into small, uniform pieces. Stir together diced fruit, currants, and lemon juice. In blender, puree syrup and mint until liquefied; pour over fruit. Add kirsch; stir to combine. Let stand at room temperature for 1 1/2 hours, stirring occasionally.

❧ Meanwhile, spread almonds on rimmed baking sheet. Place in 350°F oven for 2 minutes or until lightly toasted. Sprinkle toasted almonds over fruit mixture just before serving. Makes 4 servings.

Oranges en Surprise
(Orange Surprise)

In 1912, citrus fruits were still a rarity in northern climes, making this an exotic dessert. Although kin to baked Alaska, this cool treat is fresher and more bracing due to its tangy orange filling.

4	large navel oranges
2 cups	orange sherbet
2	egg whites
Pinch	cream of tartar
1/2 cup	fruit sugar
Dash	almond extract
	Fresh spearmint leaves
	Candied orange peel

Cut off top quarters of oranges; discard. Turn over and slice off (without penetrating flesh of oranges) the stem ends so that the oranges sit flat. Carefully spoon out flesh, reserving for another purpose. Place hollowed skins on baking sheet lined with waxed paper and freeze for 30 minutes or until rigid.

Divide sherbet evenly among oranges, firmly packing it into hollows with back of spoon. Return oranges to freezer for 30 minutes or up to 2 days.

Meanwhile, in glass bowl, using clean beaters, beat egg whites until frothy; add cream of tartar. Still beating, gradually add sugar. Continue beating for about 3 minutes or until eggs are glossy and form stiff peaks; stir in almond extract.

Remove oranges from freezer and place on baking sheet. Decoratively cover openings with meringue; use a piping bag fitted with a star tube, or spoon dollops of meringue onto oranges. Immediately bake in 425°F oven for 2 minutes, reduce temperature to 375°F and continue to bake for 3 to 5 minutes or until meringue is set and slightly browned. Garnish with spearmint leaves and candied orange peel; serve immediately. Makes 4 servings.

"I well remember that last meal on the Titanic. We had a big vase of beautiful daffodils on the table, as fresh as if they had just been picked. Everybody was gay, and people were making bets on the probable time of this record-breaking voyage."

— First-class passenger Lady Duff-Gordon

The Café Parisien

IN THE *TITANIC*'S CAFÉ PARISIEN, ONE COULD imagine oneself at a sidewalk café on a Parisian boulevard, sipping coffee or an aperitif or staving off hunger pangs with an elegant little sandwich from the circular buffet, while the sweet strains of the string trio drifted in from the reception room next door. A casual Continental atmosphere was assured by the obsequious attentions of Monsieur Gatti's well-trained staff from the adjoining à la carte restaurant. It was a place to come between meals or after dinner, a favorite resort for the younger set in first class, or those pretending to be young, such as Helen Candee and her group of gentlemen admirers, whom Colonel Gracie dubbed "our coterie." This delightful corner was unique to the *Titanic*. On the *Olympic* the space was occupied by an expanded restaurant.

Ivy-covered trellises and wicker chairs set the style for the *Titanic*'s Café Parisien.

The Verandah Café

THERE WERE ACTUALLY TWO VERAN-
dah cafés, one on each side of the
deck house just aft of the smoking
room. Considerable artifice went into
creating the illusion of an open-air verandah in a
virtually enclosed space (the opening onto the
promenade deck was sheltered from the wind).
Carefully trained ivy climbed the trellises between
the large, arched windows and white wicker furniture, evoking the outdoor terrace of a country
hotel. Just how much use these rooms received as
actual cafés is open to question. One of them
seems to have been adopted primarily as a play-
room for first-class children. But presumably,
passengers could always order a snack or a cup
of hot bouillon from an obliging steward.

The large, arched windows and trellised walls of
a popular dining room at London's Savoy Hotel
(above) may have provided the inspiration for
the *Titanic's* Verandah Café (right).

The First-Class Dining Saloon *and* Reception Room

"It was hard to realize, when dining in the large and spacious dining saloon, that one was not in some large and sumptuous hotel."

— First-class passenger Washington Dodge

LOCATED ON THE SALOON DECK AND occupying the entire width of the vessel, the first-class dining saloon was not only "by far the largest room afloat," according to *The Shipbuilder* of 1911, it was surely one of the most splendid. After descending the forward grand staircase, one entered the saloon through the spacious reception room. If the doors to the dining room had not yet been opened, one would have paused to admire the specially commissioned Aubusson tapestry depicting a medieval hunting scene, while listening to the soft strains of the *Titanic*'s orchestra gathered around the grand piano.

Upon entering the dining saloon itself, the impression would have been one of openness. The room was 92 feet wide by 114 feet long and the walls and ceiling had been painted white. Yet thanks to the unusually intimate seating—tables were for two, four, six, and eight—the warm oak furniture, the partitions breaking up the room into alcoves, and the bay windows with leaded glass, there would also have been a pleasant sense of coziness.

The Reception Room

"*The dignity and simplicity of the beautiful white paneling, delicately carved in low relief, will indeed form a fitting background to the brilliant scene when the passengers foregather before dining.*"

— *The Shipbuilder*, 1911

A steward pours tea for 1920s *Olympic* passengers in a reception room identical to the one on the *Titanic.* (Above) A White Star teapot.

The reception room on D-deck adjoined the first-class dining saloon and was where
passengers gathered before and after dinner.

The First-Class Dining Saloon

O F THE TWO MENUS THAT SURVIVE from the night of April 14, 1912, one comes from the first-class dining saloon. It is therefore possible to re-create in its entirety the sumptuous meal enjoyed by some of the ship's most renowned passengers—John Jacob Astor, Benjamin Guggenheim, Isidor and Ida Straus, the Unsinkable Molly Brown, et al. Although the menu does not label each course, it is clearly based on the classic, many-coursed meal that had evolved in France in the nineteenth century, and which Auguste Escoffier had refined and somewhat simplified.

The master, however, would indubitably have been appalled by some of the elements in this menu. For instance, he would never have begun a meal with hors d'oeuvre variés, a discordant cacophony of bite-size bits, usually served from a trolley, and including various pickled items whose astringent flavors only clash with the dishes to come. The raw oysters, on the other hand, made the ideal beginning to such a meal. Furthermore, at the Ritz, no meat would ever

A first-class dinner menu (right), shown with its cover, from the night of April 14, 1912, clearly follows the classic pattern laid down by Escoffier and his disciples.

R.M.S. "TITANIC" RESTAURANT RECEPTION ROOM.

R.M.S. "TITANIC."

APRIL 14, 1912

HORS D'ŒUVRE VARIÈS
OYSTERS

CONSOMMÉ OLGA   CREAM OF BARLEY

SALMON, MOUSSELINE SAUCE, CUCUMBER

FILET MIGNONS LILI
SAUTÉ OF CHICKEN, LYONNAISE
VEGETABLE MARROW FARCIE

LAMB, MINT SAUCE
ROAST DUCKLING, APPLE SAUCE
SIRLOIN OF BEEF CHATEAU POTATOES

GREEN PEAS   CREAMED CARROTS
BOILED RICE
PARMENTIER & BOILED NEW POTATOES

PUNCH ROMAINE

ROAST SQUAB & CRESS
COLD ASPARAGUS VINAIGRETTE
PÂTE DE FOIE GRAS
CELERY

WALDORF PUDDING
PEACHES IN CHARTREUSE JELLY
CHOCOLATE & VANILLA ECLAIRS
FRENCH ICE CREAM

First-Class Menu

FIRST COURSE — HORS D'OEUVRE
Canapés à l'Amiral
Oysters à la Russe

White Bordeaux, White Burgundy or
Chablis (especially with oysters)

SECOND COURSE — SOUPS
Consommé Olga
Cream of Barley Soup

Madeira or Sherry

THIRD COURSE — FISH
Poached Salmon with Mousseline Sauce

Dry Rhine or Moselle

FOURTH COURSE — ENTRÉES
Filets Mignons Lili
Chicken Lyonnaise
Vegetable Marrow Farci

Red Bordeaux

FIFTH COURSE — REMOVES
Lamb with Mint Sauce
Calvados-Glazed Roast Duckling
with Applesauce
Roast Sirloin of Beef Forestière
Château Potatoes
Minted Green Pea Timbales
Creamed Carrots
Boiled Rice
Parmentier and Boiled New Potatoes

Red Burgundy or Beaujolais

SIXTH COURSE — PUNCH OR SORBET
Punch Romaine

SEVENTH COURSE — ROAST
Roasted Squab on Wilted Cress

Red Burgundy

EIGHTH COURSE — SALAD
Asparagus Salad with Champagne-
Saffron Vinaigrette

NINTH COURSE — COLD DISH
Pâté de Foie Gras
Celery

Sauterne or Sweet Rhine Wine

TENTH COURSE — SWEETS
Waldorf Pudding
Peaches in Chartreuse Jelly
Chocolate Painted Eclairs
with French Vanilla Cream
French Vanilla Ice Cream

Sweet Dessert Wines (Muscatel, Tokay, Sauterne)

ELEVENTH COURSE — DESSERT
Assorted fresh fruits and cheeses

Sweet Dessert Wines, Champagne, or Sparkling Wine

AFTER DINNER
Coffee, cigars

Port or Cordials

> *"Stomachs have shrunk, for no one today could eat the meals that were swallowed as a matter of course fifty years ago."*
>
> — Noel Streatfeild in 1956

have been presented without an individual garnish appropriate to its character. Here the removes course has veered perilously close to the meat, potato, and vegetable main dish of a more middle-class dinner. Undoubtedly, these slight vulgarizations reflect the less-educated palates of the *Titanic*'s predominately Anglo-American clientele. But despite such cavils, the final meal in first class was a splendid and overabundant feast.

That night there appear to have been eleven separate courses, including dessert, most providing a selection of more than one delicacy. (In a slight departure from the norm, the entrées precede the removes; usually the order 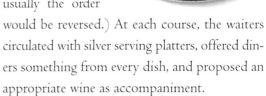 would be reversed.) At each course, the waiters circulated with silver serving platters, offered diners something from every dish, and proposed an appropriate wine as accompaniment.

The only known photograph of the *Titanic*'s dining saloon (left) is believed to show the scene at luncheon on April 11. This elegant cup and saucer (above) was a presentation piece prior to the sailing.

SUGGESTED SHORTER MENU
FOR FIRST CLASS

Those interested in re-creating the first-class dinner as accurately as possible, but who balk at the sheer number of courses and quantity of food, may want to attempt an abbreviated version. Here's what we suggest:

FIRST COURSE — SOUP

Consommé Olga

Cream of Barley Soup

❧

SECOND COURSE — FISH

Poached Salmon with Mousseline Sauce

❧

THIRD COURSE — ENTRÉES

Filet Mignons Lili

Chicken Lyonnaise

Vegetable Marrow Farci

❧

FOURTH COURSE — PUNCH

Punch Romaine

❧

FIFTH COURSE — ROAST

Roasted Squab on Wilted Cress

❧

SIXTH COURSE — SALAD

Asparagus Salad with Champagne-Saffron Vinaigrette

❧

SEVENTH COURSE — SWEETS

Waldorf Pudding

Peaches in Chartreuse Jelly

Chocolate Painted Eclairs with French Vanilla Cream

How much of this marathon menu did people actually eat? We can't know for sure. We do know that upper-crust Edwardians regularly sat down to meals that followed this opulent and time-consuming ritual. If the *Titanic's* menu looks daunting to a modern stomach, that's because it is. You can re-create the experience without committing gastronomic suicide by serving each course in small portions and drinking only a small glass of wine with each. In fact, we found such a meal an amazingly digestible sensory cornucopia. But plan to serve it on a night when you can sleep late the following morning.

To keep things as simple as possible, we recommend that you choose only one dish from each course and do so with an eye to variety. If your entrée is the chicken Lyonnaise, then choose as your remove either the roast lamb or the sirloin.

You will want to prepare some dishes in the preceding days, and you will need to set aside a full day for the final cooking—ideally with a trusty sous-chef to help you—and do preliminary work on every dish ahead of time so that as the meal unfolds you need only finish each dish off and serve it to your admiring guests. (See Make-Ahead Chart on pages 92 and 93.)

The actual first-class menu doesn't describe the first course in detail, identifying only "hors d'oeuvre variés" and "oysters." We have substituted canapés à l'amiral, an Escoffier standard. (For other hors d'oeuvre possibilities, consult a classic French cookbook.) Oysters must have formed part of many a first-class meal, given that the *Titanic* carried 1,221 quarts of them when it left Southampton. The recipe we've chosen, oysters à la Russe, presumably takes its name from the addition of vodka to a piquant relish. But if you're a stickler for accuracy, serve them raw and unadorned on the half shell, which is likely how they were served on the last night.

Canapés à l'Amiral

1/2	thin baguette
1 tsp	lime juice
10	small shrimp, halved lengthwise, cooked
	Fresh flat-leaf (Italian) parsley
2 tbsp	flying fish roe
	SHRIMP BUTTER
1 tbsp	vegetable oil
1	large shallot, minced
1	clove garlic, minced
8 oz	shrimp in shell
1/4 cup	brandy
4 oz	cream cheese, softened
2 tbsp	butter, softened
1 tbsp	tomato paste
1/4 tsp	each salt and pepper
Dash	vanilla

SHRIMP BUTTER: In skillet, heat oil over medium heat; add shallot and garlic; cook, stirring often, for 5 minutes or until softened. Increase heat to high, add shrimp and sauté, stirring, for 3 to 4 minutes or until shells are pink and flesh is opaque. Transfer shrimp and vegetables to bowl of food processor. Return pan to stove and pour in brandy; cook, stirring, for 30 seconds or until brandy is reduced to a glaze; scrape into shrimp mixture.

❦ Puree shrimp mixture until finely chopped. Add cream cheese, butter, tomato paste, salt, pepper, and vanilla. Process until almost smooth. Press shrimp mixture through coarse sieve set over bowl; discard shells.

❦ Slice baguette into 20 thin slices. Place on baking sheet and toast under broiler for 1 minute per side or until lightly golden. Reserve.

❦ Drizzle lime juice over cooked shrimp halves; stir and reserve.

❦ Place shrimp butter in piping bag fitted with star tube. Pipe shrimp butter onto toasts. (Alternatively, using a table knife, spread shrimp mixture onto toasts.) Top with a cooked shrimp half and a parsley leaf. Top each canapé with an equal amount of flying fish roe. Makes 20 hors d'oeuvre.

Note: We suggest flying fish roe for color, economy, and taste. (This may be called tapiko by some fish vendors.) Though crawfish roe may have been used on the Titanic, *the more likely choice was sturgeon roe (caviar).*

Oysters à la Russe

2 tbsp	vodka
1/2 tsp	lemon juice
1/4 tsp	prepared horseradish
Dash	hot pepper sauce
Pinch	each granulated sugar and salt
1	plum tomato, seeded and finely chopped
1 tbsp	finely chopped chives
12	large oysters
	Coarsely cracked black peppercorns

In bowl, stir together vodka, lemon juice, horseradish, hot pepper sauce, sugar, and salt. Gently stir in tomato and chives.

🍇 Wash oysters under running water to remove any loose barnacles or sand. Insert tip of oyster shucker between shell halves near hinge; twist upward to open shell. Discard top shell. Using blade of shucker, sever connective membrane that holds oyster to bottom shell. Place open oysters on bed of shaved or crushed ice.

🍇 Spoon vodka relish over each oyster; dust with cracked pepper. Makes 6 servings.

Menus of the day usually offered a choice of one clear soup and one thick soup. Here, a beef consommé is paired with a light-tasting cream of barley.

Consommé Olga

A woman named Olga may have inspired an actual chef; more likely hers was a generic
Russian name used to indicate that this dish has a Russian flavor. The ingredient that originally
distinguished this soup from ordinary beef consommé was vésiga, the dried spinal marrow of a sturgeon.
However, vésiga is very difficult to find today, even at the best gourmet shops. On the Titanic, it would
have been soaked in water for up to five hours, boiled in bouillon for another three until it resembled
gelatin, then sliced and floated in the piping hot consommé. We have substituted sea scallops,
which are similar in texture and considerably more flavorful.

7 cups	degreased veal or beef stock
1	each carrot, leek, and celery stalk, finely chopped
1/2	tomato, chopped
1 tbsp	chopped parsley stems
1/4 lb	lean ground veal or beef
1/4 tsp	each salt and pepper
3	egg whites, beaten until frothy
1/4 cup	port
	GARNISH
6	large sea scallops
1/2	celeriac bulb or head of celery, blanched and julienned
1/4	English cucumber, seeded and julienned

In tall narrow pot, gently heat stock until body temperature. Meanwhile, in large bowl, stir together vegetables, parsley, and meat until well combined; add salt and pepper; fold in egg whites.

 Whisk heated stock into egg mixture; return to pot and, whisking, bring slowly to boil. When mixture begins to look frothy, stop stirring to allow egg mixture to rise and solidify into a raft. Lower heat to medium-low. Carefully make a vent hole in raft with spoon handle. Simmer consommé gently for 30 minutes.

 Leaving pot on heat, carefully push raft down with back of ladle; ladle clarified consommé through cheesecloth-lined sieve into clean pot. Heat until very hot. Stir in port.

 GARNISH: Slice scallops crosswise into 3 pieces, place 3 discs into bottom of each of 6 warmed bowls. Pour hot consommé over scallops; arrange celeriac and cucumber decoratively in each bowl. Serve immediately. Makes 6 servings.

Cream of Barley Soup

This traditional French country favorite can be served at any consistency from chunky to smooth.
We recommend something halfway between a smooth puree and a barely blended version.

I tbsp	vegetable oil
1/4 cup	finely chopped salt pork or bacon
2	each carrots and onions, finely chopped
3	cloves garlic, minced
I	bay leaf
2 tsp	coarsely chopped parsley stems
1/4 tsp	peppercorns
I cup	pearl barley
7 cups	beef or other meat stock
I cup	whipping cream
2 tbsp	whiskey
I tbsp	red wine vinegar
	Salt and pepper

In large pot, heat oil over medium heat; add salt pork and cook, stirring often, for 2 minutes. Stir in carrot, onion, and garlic; cover and cook, stirring occasionally, for 10 minutes or until vegetables are very soft.

🍇 Meanwhile, wrap bay leaf, parsley stems, and peppercorns in cheesecloth; fold over and tie to make bouquet garni. Stir barley into vegetable mixture; cook, stirring, for about 45 seconds. Pour in stock and add bouquet garni. Bring to boil. Reduce heat to low and simmer, covered, for 40 to 45 minutes or until barley is tender.

🍇 Remove from heat; in blender or food processor, puree soup in batches until almost smooth. Transfer to clean pot; cook over medium heat until steaming. Whisk in cream, whiskey, and vinegar. Season with salt and pepper to taste. Do not boil. Makes 6 to 8 servings.

Poached Salmon with Mousseline Sauce

The menu for the last dinner contains only one fish entry, but it is an unbeatable one: lightly poached Atlantic salmon topped with a rich mousseline sauce and garnished with sliced cucumbers. A mousseline sauce is simply a classic hollandaise to which some whipped cream has been added. (The fresh dill we suggest may not be strictly to period but does enhance the flavor.)

6 cups	Basic Court Bouillon (recipe follows)
6	salmon fillets or steaks (8 oz each)
30	very thin slices English cucumber
6	sprigs fresh dill (optional)

MOUSSELINE SAUCE

2/3 cup	melted unsalted butter
3 tbsp	water
3	egg yolks
1/4 tsp	each salt and white pepper
1 tbsp	lemon juice
2 tbsp	chopped fresh dill (optional)
1/4 cup	lightly whipped cream

BASIC COURT BOUILLON

7 cups	water
1	carrot, sliced
1	small onion, chopped
6	peppercorns
1	bay leaf
1/4 cup	parsley stems
1 tsp	salt
1 1/4 cups	dry white wine (or 3/4 cup white vinegar)

In large shallow pot, heat court bouillon until just below boiling point. Using slotted spoon or spatula, gently place salmon into bouillon (adding, if necessary, up to 1 cup boiling water to cover fish completely). Poach fish for 3 to 5 minutes or until opaque on the outside but still coral-colored in center.

❦ MOUSSELINE SAUCE: Meanwhile, using spoon, skim froth from surface of melted butter and discard. Allow butter to cool slightly.

❦ In top of double boiler or heatproof bowl, whisk water and egg yolks together with salt and pepper for 30 seconds or until pale yellow and frothy. Over barely simmering water, whisk mixture for 3 minutes or until it draws a ribbon for 5 seconds.

❦ Remove pan from heat; whisk in warm butter, 1 tbsp at a time, until sauce begins to thicken. Still whisking, pour remaining butter into sauce in a slow, steady stream. Stir in lemon juice and dill (if using). Remove from heat; cool slightly. Gently fold in whipped cream. Adjust seasoning to taste. Keep warm by setting over a pot of warm water.

❦ Arrange poached salmon on warmed plates. Spoon sauce down center of each piece of fish so that a border of flesh remains visible. Garnish each plate with a cucumber fan and a sprig of fresh dill (if using). Makes 6 servings.

Tips: If using salmon steaks, skewer ends together with a toothpick before poaching. To make an easy but lovely garnish, bend cucumber slices in half and skewer through the center onto a toothpick. Space evenly to create a ruffle. Enjoy this dish hot or cold.

Basic Court Bouillon

❦ In pot, bring water, carrot, onion, peppercorns, bay leaf, parsley stems, salt, and wine or vinegar to boil over high heat. Reduce heat and simmer for 30 minutes. Strain. (Keeps, tightly covered in refrigerator, for up to 1 week.)

Unlike the entrée on a modern restaurant menu, the classic entrée is a small portion of a very choice dish, a chance for the kitchen to really strut its stuff. Here, we present the chicken recipe before the richer filets mignons. The stuffed vegetable marrow would have been considered a separate entrée, not a side dish.

Chicken Lyonnaise

This is one of the most delicious items on the first-class dinner menu. The sauce is from Lyons, considered by many to be the gastronomic capital of France, and employs two foods for which the area is renowned— onions from the Rhone Valley and poultry from Bresse.

&

1/3 cup	all-purpose flour
2 tbsp	chopped fresh thyme (or 1 tbsp dried)
1/2 tsp	each salt and pepper
6	boneless chicken breasts
1	egg, beaten
3 tbsp	vegetable oil
2	onions, thinly sliced
1	clove garlic, minced
1/3 cup	white wine
1 cup	chicken stock
2 tsp	tomato paste
Pinch	granulated sugar

In sturdy plastic bag, shake together flour, 1 tbsp of the thyme (or 1 1/2 tsp if using dried), salt, and pepper. One at a time, dip chicken breasts into egg, and then shake in flour mixture.

In large deep skillet, heat 2 tbsp of the vegetable oil over medium-high heat. Place chicken in pan, skin side down. Cook, turning once, for 10 minutes or until golden brown. Remove from skillet and place in 225°F oven.

Reduce heat to medium; add remaining oil to skillet. Stir in onions, garlic, and remaining thyme; cook, stirring often, for 5 minutes or until onions are translucent. Increase heat to medium-high and continue to cook onions, stirring often, for 5 minutes or until golden brown.

Add wine to pan; cook, stirring to scrape up any brown bits, for about 1 minute or until reduced by half. Stir in stock, tomato paste, and sugar. Boil for 2 minutes or until beginning to thicken. Return chicken to pan, turning to coat, and cook for 5 minutes or until juices from chicken run clear. Makes 6 servings.

On later White Star liners, passengers were summoned to dinner by the ringing of a gong rather than the sounding of a bugle.

Filets Mignons Lili

If you are looking for a dish that epitomizes the excess of the Edwardian era, look no further: a filet mignon accompanied by a buttery wine sauce, topped with a piece of foie gras and a truffle, and set on a bed of buttery potatoes Anna. (If you are serving all eleven courses, it would probably be wise to save this for another occasion.) Most specialty butchers will be able to provide foie gras if you give them advance notice. Truffles are even more precious, which is why we've made them optional in our version of the recipe.

6	filets mignons (2 ¹/₂ lb)
¹/₂ tsp	each salt and pepper
I tbsp	each butter and vegetable oil
2	cloves garlic, sliced
6	foie gras (goose liver) medallions
6	cooked artichoke hearts, quartered
6	slices black truffle (optional)

SAUCE

2 tbsp	butter
3	large shallots or ¹/₂ onion, finely chopped
I ¹/₂ tbsp	tomato paste
I	bay leaf
I	sprig fresh rosemary
¹/₂ cup	each cognac, Madeira, and red wine
3 cups	homemade beef stock
	Salt and pepper

POTATOES ANNA

³/₄ cup	melted unsalted butter
6	medium baking potatoes, peeled and very thinly sliced
I tsp	each salt and pepper

SAUCE: In saucepan, melt I tbsp of the butter over medium heat; add shallots and cook, stirring often, for 5 minutes or until softened. Stir in tomato paste, bay leaf, and rosemary until well combined. Stir in cognac, Madeira, and red wine; bring to boil. Boil for 10 minutes or until reduced to about ¹/₂ cup. Stir in beef stock. Boil for 15 minutes or until reduced to about I cup. Strain into clean pot set over low heat and whisk in remaining butter. Season to taste. Keep warm.

❦ POTATOES ANNA: Brush 11-inch oven-proof skillet with enough melted butter to coat. Arrange potatoes in overlapping circles, brushing each layer with enough butter to coat; sprinkle each layer with some of the salt and pepper; press top layer gently down. Place pan over medium-high heat for about 10 minutes or until bottom is browned. Cover and bake in 450°F oven for 15 minutes or until potatoes are tender and lightly browned on top. Broil for I to 2 minutes or until brown and crisp. Let stand for 5 minutes.

❦ Meanwhile, sprinkle meat with salt and pepper. In large skillet, melt butter with vegetable oil over medium heat; add garlic and cook, stirring often, for 2 minutes; increase heat to medium-high and add filets mignons. Cook, turning once, for 10 to 12 minutes or until well browned but still pink in middle. Remove from pan and let stand, tented with foil, for about 5 minutes. Wipe out pan and return to high heat. Add foie gras and cook for 30 seconds per side or until golden brown. Remove from pan and reserve. Gently toss artichokes in pan juices and cook for 2 minutes or until heated through.

❦ Cut cooked potato round into 6 portions and place I piece, upside down, on each of 6 heated plates; top with a filet mignon, followed by a slice of foie gras, and a truffle slice (if using). Ladle sauce around edge of plate; garnish with artichokes. Makes 6 servings.

Tips: Because this sauce is a reduction, the beef stock must be homemade if the sauce is to thicken properly. It is better to use two skillets to cook the meat than to crowd the filets.

Vegetable Marrow Farci

*Since vegetable marrows are available for only a few weeks each year, feel free to
substitute two large zucchini (courgettes). Before the Second World War, the stuffing would have been
made with short-grain rice, which is now difficult to find. Unless you are a stickler for Titanic accuracy,
sushi rice or long-grain rice make perfectly acceptable substitutes.*

1	vegetable marrow or 2 large zucchini
2 tbsp	olive oil
1 cup	finely chopped red onion
3	cloves garlic, minced
1/4 cup	chopped fresh basil
1 tsp	dried oregano
1 tbsp	tomato paste
1 1/2 cups	button mushrooms, chopped
2 tbsp	red wine vinegar
2/3 cup	cooked rice
1/4 tsp	each salt and pepper
1/4 cup	grated Parmesan cheese
1/4 cup	fresh bread crumbs
2 tbsp	butter, melted
	Fresh basil

Halve marrow lengthwise; scoop out flesh with spoon leaving 1/4-inch shell. Discard large seeds. Chop scooped flesh into small dice; reserve.

In skillet, heat oil over medium heat; add onion and garlic and cook, stirring often, for 7 to 8 minutes or until softened and lightly browned. Stir in basil, oregano, reserved marrow, and tomato paste. Cook, stirring often, for 5 minutes; increase heat to high and add mushrooms. Cook, stirring, for 3 minutes or until vegetables are well browned; stir in vinegar. Remove from heat and cool slightly. Stir in rice, salt, pepper, and 3 tbsp of the cheese.

Spoon into hollowed vegetables, packing lightly with back of spoon. Sprinkle evenly with bread crumbs and remaining cheese; drizzle with butter. Place in greased baking dish in 350°F oven for 30 to 40 minutes or until marrow is fork-tender and topping is well browned.

To serve, slice marrow diagonally in 3-inch slices. Garnish with fresh basil. Makes 6 servings.

A White Star napkin ring that once belonged to Herbert Pitman,
Third Officer on the *Titanic*.

In the choreography of an Edwardian meal, a lighter course generally followed a heavier one. With the remove, we reach the solid center of the *Titanic's* last dinner. It is the only course that closely resembles the main course served in a restaurant today. The *Titanic's* last dinner included three selections—roast lamb, roast duck, and roast sirloin. We have not given detailed recipes for three items appearing on the first-class dinner menu, "Boiled Rice" and "Parmentier and Boiled New Potatoes." Escoffier recommends Carolina long-grain rice to accompany a meal such as this one, but any long-grain rice will do. The new potatoes would have been cubed and boiled, then served with butter. Parmentier potatoes are made from cubed raw potatoes, browned in butter and tossed with chives.

Lamb with Mint Sauce

Both lamb and mutton appear on the Titanic's *menus, the latter generally reserved for luncheon. Lamb appealed more to American diners who, even today, eat less lamb than the British and would have found mutton unpalatable.*

1	leg of lamb (3 1/2 to 4 lb)
2	cloves garlic, minced
3 tbsp	olive oil
2 tbsp	chopped fresh rosemary
I tsp	Dijon mustard
2 tsp	freshly ground pepper
1/4 cup	white wine
1/2 tsp	salt
	MINT SAUCE
2	shallots, minced
1/4 cup	white wine
I cup	chicken stock
2 tsp	cider vinegar
I tsp	granulated sugar
1/4 cup	chopped fresh mint (or I tbsp dried mint flakes)
	Fresh mint sprigs

Trim lamb of gristle and excess fat. Stir together garlic, 2 tbsp of the oil, rosemary, mustard and pepper; rub over surface of meat; marinate at room temperature for I hour or in refrigerator for up to 48 hours. In large heavy skillet, heat remaining oil over high heat; add leg and sear, turning often, for about 5 minutes or until well browned on every side.

Place leg in roasting pan. Pour wine and salt into skillet and bring to boil, stirring to scrape up any brown bits; pour over meat. Cook lamb in 450°F oven for 15 minutes; reduce heat to 350°F and continue to roast for 25 minutes for a rare roast (125°F on instant-read meat thermometer) or for 35 minutes for medium-rare (140°F on instant-read meat thermometer). Remove roast from pan and tent with foil; let rest for 15 minutes.

MINT SAUCE: Meanwhile, place roasting pan over medium heat. Stir in shallots and cook, stirring often, for 5 minutes or until softened. Stir in wine; bring to boil and cook, stirring, for I minute or until reduced to a glaze. Stir in stock, vinegar, and sugar. Continue to boil rapidly for 2 minutes or until sauce is slightly thickened; pour through fine-meshed sieve. Stir in mint. Serve sauce alongside roast. Garnish with fresh mint sprigs. Makes 6 servings.

Calvados-Glazed Roast Duckling with Applesauce

The last dinner menu makes no mention of a glaze for the duck, but glazing was, and remains, a common culinary grace note for roast fowl.

1	duckling (4 lb)
1 tbsp	chopped fresh thyme
1/2 tsp	each salt and pepper
2	shallots, halved
1	small tart apple, quartered
1/2 cup	chicken stock
1/2 cup	Calvados or apple cider
1/2 cup	brown sugar

APPLESAUCE

1 tbsp	vegetable oil
2	small shallots, finely chopped
1 tsp	granulated sugar
1 tsp	cider vinegar
2	tart apples, peeled, cored, and chopped

Remove giblets and neck from duck; rinse and pat dry, inside and out. Trim excess fat from both ends of cavity. In small bowl, stir together thyme, salt, and pepper; rub all over duck, inside and out. Place shallots and apple inside cavity. Using poultry pins or basting needle, truss cavity closed. Twist wing tips behind back.

❦ Place duck, breast side up, on rack in large roasting pan. Roast in 425°F oven for 30 minutes. Shield breast meat with foil, reduce heat to 350°F and bake for 1 hour or until instant-read meat thermometer registers 180°F when inserted into leg. Place on heated platter.

❦ Set roasting pan on stove over medium-high heat; skim off fat. Stir in chicken stock and Calvados; bring to boil, stirring to scrape up any brown bits. Boil for 5 minutes or until reduced to 1/2 cup. Stir in sugar and continue to cook for 3 to 5 minutes or until slightly syrupy. Pour into heatproof bowl.

❦ Return duck to roasting pan; remove foil and brush with half the glaze. Bake in 350°F oven for 5 minutes and brush with remaining glaze. Roast for 20 minutes longer. Increase heat to 475°F and cook for 5 minutes or until skin is well browned and crisp. Remove to heated platter; tent with foil and let rest for 20 minutes. Makes 2 servings, but can be doubled or tripled easily in a large oven.

❦ APPLESAUCE: Meanwhile, in heavy-bottomed saucepan, heat oil over medium heat; add shallots and cook for 5 minutes or until softened. Sprinkle sugar over shallots; cook, stirring often, for 5 minutes or until shallots are well browned and very soft. Stir in vinegar and apples. Cover and cook for 7 to 8 minutes or until apples are tender. Mash until smooth.

❦ Serve applesauce alongside duckling. Makes 2 servings. Doubles or triples easily.

Roast Sirloin of Beef Forestière

*Unlike the chefs on the Titanic, you won't need to roast a whole sirloin.
A large two-inch thick sirloin steak will do nicely. As garnish we've added a sauce forestière, a classic gravy
with wild mushrooms and onions. This sauce had certainly been invented by 1912, but we have no way of
knowing what sauce actually accompanied the "sirloin of beef" announced on the menu.*

1/3 cup	red wine
2 tbsp	vegetable oil
1 tbsp	chopped fresh thyme (or 2 tsp dried)
1	small onion, finely chopped
2	cloves garlic, minced
1	2-inch thick sirloin steak (2 lb)
1/2 tsp	each salt and pepper
12	pearl onions, blanched

SAUCE FORESTIÈRE

2 oz	side bacon cut in lardons
2 1/2 cups	sliced wild mushrooms in season
1/2 cup	red wine
2	sprigs fresh thyme (or 1/4 tsp dried)
1	bay leaf
1 1/2 cups	beef or chicken stock
1 tbsp	butter
1/4 tsp	each salt and pepper

In large, shallow baking dish, combine wine, vegetable oil, thyme, onion, and garlic. Add steak, turning to coat well; cover and marinate at room temperature for at least 30 minutes or for up to 24 hours in the refrigerator (bring to room temperature 30 minutes before cooking).

❧ Remove steak from dish. Season with salt and pepper and place in roasting pan; add onions. Roast in 425°F oven for 20 minutes; reduce temperature to 375°F and continue to roast for 15 minutes for medium doneness (internal temperature 130°F). When cooked, remove sirloin and onions from pan and rest, tented with foil, for 10 minutes.

❧ SAUCE FORESTIÈRE: Meanwhile, in small skillet, cook bacon lardons over high heat for 5 minutes or until crisp and brown; remove from pan and reserve. Drain off all but 2 tbsp fat; stir in mushrooms and cook, stirring gently, for 3 to 5 minutes or until browned. Remove from pan and add to bacon.

❧ Stir in wine, thyme sprigs, and bay leaf. Bring to boil; cook for 7 minutes or until reduced to about 2 tbsp. Reserve. Place roasting pan on burner set to medium-high. Pour beef stock into pan, stirring to scrape up brown bits; bring to boil. Simmer for 3 minutes or until beginning to thicken. Stir in reserved wine glaze, butter, mushrooms, bacon, salt, and pepper. Heat through; remove bay leaf and thyme sprigs.

❧ Thinly slice sirloin across the grain and serve garnished with onions and sauce. Makes 6 to 8 servings.

Château Potatoes

Called "château" because they were a country favorite of French nobility, these would go well with any of the removes.
Chefs of the day used turning knives (crescent-moon-bladed paring knives) to cut the potatoes into eight-sided jewel shapes.

6	medium potatoes
2 tbsp	unsalted butter
I tbsp	vegetable oil
I tbsp	finely chopped fresh rosemary leaves
$^1/_2$ tsp	each salt and pepper

Peel potatoes; using a turning knife, cut into eight-sided jewel shapes (alternatively, cut into thick, evenly shaped wedges). Meanwhile, place butter, oil, and rosemary in large, rimmed baking sheet. Set pan in 425°F oven for 2 to 3 minutes or until butter is sizzling.

❦ Pat potatoes dry; place in heated pan and stir to coat with butter mixture. Bake in 425°F oven, stirring occasionally, for 35 to 40 minutes or until potatoes are golden brown. Season with salt and pepper. Makes 6 servings.

Minted Green Pea Timbales

Contrary to modern custom, the Edwardians seldom left a good vegetable to stand on its own merits.
But of all the classic French variations on vegetables, the timbale is surely one of the most delicious.

I tbsp	salt
4 cups	peas, fresh or frozen (thawed)
2 $^1/_2$ tbsp	chopped fresh mint (or I tsp dried)
$^1/_4$ tsp	granulated sugar
$^1/_4$ tsp	pepper
3	egg whites
$^1/_2$ cup	whipping cream
	Fresh mint sprigs
	Sour cream or crème fraîche

In large saucepan of boiling water, dissolve all but $^1/_4$ tsp of the salt. Add peas and blanch for 2 minutes. Drain and rinse under cold water until chilled through; drain well.

❦ Place peas, mint, sugar, remaining salt, and pepper in blender or food processor; puree until very smooth. With motor running, add egg whites one at a time; pour in cream and blend until well combined.

❦ Divide pea mixture among 6 greased $^1/_2$-cup ramekins or custard cups lined with parchment rounds. Place ramekins in baking pan; pour in enough boiling water to come halfway up sides of dishes. Cover with foil and, using sharp knife, make vent holes at random intervals; bake in 350°F oven for about 30 minutes or until tester inserted into center of timbale comes out clean. Let rest for 2 to 3 minutes; run knife around edge of each dish and turn timbales out onto warmed plates. Remove parchment rounds.

❦ Garnish with a sprig of mint and a dollop of sour cream. Makes 6 servings.

Creamed Carrots

The standard in Edwardian times was to cook vegetables until soft. Here, as a concession to modern tastes,
we recommend cooking the carrots until easily pierced by a fork.

8 or 9	medium carrots, julienned
1	cinnamon stick (or 1 tsp ground cinnamon)
1 tbsp	butter
1/2 tsp	salt
1/2 tsp	ground cinnamon
1/4 tsp	ground nutmeg
Pinch	pepper
1 tsp	lemon juice
1/3 cup	whipping cream
2 tbsp	finely chopped fresh chives

Place carrots in medium saucepan with enough water to cover; add cinnamon stick. Bring to boil, reduce heat to medium-high, and cook for 6 to 8 minutes or until carrots are fork-tender. Drain, remove cinnamon stick, and return carrots to pan. Add butter, salt, ground cinnamon, nutmeg, and pepper; mix well. Add lemon juice and cream; boil for 1 minute or until cream is slightly thickened.

❦ Adjust seasoning if necessary. Turn into shallow serving bowl; sprinkle with chives and serve. Makes 6 servings.

SIXTH COURSE — PUNCH OR SORBET

Punch Romaine

Escoffier popularized this form of alcoholic ice as a palate cleanser. Like a modern sorbet,
it would have been served in dessert cups and eaten with a spoon.

6 cups	crushed ice
1 cup	Simple Syrup (see page 53)
2 cups	champagne or sparkling wine
1 cup	white wine
1/3 cup	freshly squeezed orange juice
2 tbsp	lemon juice
2 tbsp	white rum (optional)
	Orange peel, slivered

In blender, combine crushed ice, simple syrup, champagne, white wine, orange juice, and lemon juice. Blend until well combined.

❦ Spoon mixture into individual dessert cups; drizzle with white rum (if using) and garnish with a sliver of orange peel. Serve immediately. Makes 8 servings.

After the pause provided by the punch comes the roast, preferably game fowl but domestic poultry will do. If you are looking for a course to cut in order to make your meal slightly less of a marathon, don't choose the roast. As culinary historian Jean-Paul Aron has written, "in the polyphony of the gourmet, [the roast] is the chorale: one can imagine it being played on the organ."

Roasted Squab on Wilted Cress

Squab, a small game bird, is still relatively common in Europe where it has been a popular dish since the Middle Ages. In North America, where squab is expensive and difficult to find, partridge makes an acceptable substitute. Wilted cress is a modern affectation, though a tasty one. On the Titanic *the roast would have been served with a simple garnish of fresh watercress.*

6	squab or partridge (1 lb each)
1 tbsp	olive or vegetable oil
3	cloves garlic, minced
1 tbsp	chopped fresh marjoram (or 1 tsp dried)
$^1/_2$ tsp	each salt and pepper
6	slices side bacon
$^3/_4$ cup	each Madeira, red wine, and chicken stock

WILTED WATERCRESS

3 tbsp	walnut oil
2	cloves garlic, minced
20 cups	rinsed watercress
1 $^1/_2$ tsp	lemon juice
$^1/_2$ tsp	each salt and pepper

Rinse and pat dry squab, inside and out.

In bowl, mix together oil, garlic, marjoram, salt, and pepper. Rub over squab, inside and out. Truss and secure a bacon slice over each squab breast. Place in roasting pan and cook in 450°F oven for 15 to 20 minutes or until juices run pink. Remove and discard bacon and broil for 2 to 3 minutes or until well browned. Remove from pan; tent with foil and let rest for 10 minutes.

Meanwhile, place roasting pan over high heat. Stir in Madeira, red wine, and chicken stock. Bring to boil, stirring to scrape up any brown bits; cook for 7 to 8 minutes or until reduced to about $^1/_2$ cup. Strain and keep warm.

WILTED WATERCRESS: In large pot, heat 2 tbsp of the walnut oil over medium heat. Add garlic and cook, stirring, for 2 minutes; increase heat to high and add damp watercress. Cook, stirring, for 1 minute or until wilted. Toss with lemon juice, salt, pepper, and remaining walnut oil.

Make a nest of watercress on heated platter; halve each squab, removing backbone, and arrange over top; serve with sauce on side. Makes 6 servings.

On an Escoffier menu, a salad course often followed the roast. In general, salads and vegetable dishes were served separately, not on the same plate as a meat dish.

Asparagus Salad with Champagne-Saffron Vinaigrette

On the Titanic, *the asparagus would have been presented in elongated dishes and served with special asparagus tongs.*

I $^1/_2$ lb	asparagus
$^1/_4$ tsp	saffron threads
I $^1/_2$ tbsp	champagne vinegar or white wine vinegar
$^1/_2$ tsp	Dijon mustard
Pinch	granulated sugar
3 tbsp	extra virgin olive oil
	Salt and pepper
$^1/_2$	sweet red or yellow pepper, finely diced
	Lettuce

Holding asparagus halfway up stalk, snap off woody ends at natural breaking point and discard. In wide, deep skillet or large pot of boiling salted water, cook asparagus for 3 to 5 minutes or until tender but not limp. Drain and run under cold water until completely cooled; drain well.

Meanwhile, in large bowl, stir saffron into I tsp boiling water; let stand for 2 minutes or until softened. Stir in champagne vinegar, mustard and sugar. Whisking, drizzle in olive oil. Season with salt and pepper to taste. Add asparagus and diced pepper; toss to coat. Arrange on lettuce-lined serving platter. Makes 6 servings.

This course often included a cold roast or boned turkey or foie gras—the case here. At the last dinner, the foie gras was served with celery, probably presented unadorned as a textural contrast to the rich foie gras. The foie gras would have been marinated in Madeira, enhanced with truffles and baked en croûte. A more practical and affordable substitute would be a fine pâté served on thin toast.

In many Edwardian meals, hot sweets and cold sweets would have appeared as separate courses. Here they seem to have been offered at the same time. The ice cream, which sometimes also functioned as a second pause after the roast, may here have accompanied one of the other sweets or have been served solo.

Waldorf Pudding

*Of the many authentic Edwardian recipes we researched for this book, Waldorf pudding was
one that eluded us. The recipe here is a modern invention based on three of the essential ingredients in the
famous Waldorf salad—walnuts, raisins, and apples.*

2	large tart apples, peeled
1/2 cup	sultana (golden) raisins
1 tbsp	lemon juice
1 tbsp	finely chopped crystallized ginger
1 tbsp	butter
1/3 cup	granulated sugar
2 cups	milk
4	egg yolks, beaten
Pinch	freshly ground nutmeg
1 tsp	pure vanilla extract
1/4 cup	toasted walnuts, halved

Thinly slice apples. Stir in raisins, lemon juice, and ginger. In skillet, melt butter over high heat; add apple mixture and cook for 1 minute. Stir in 2 tbsp of the sugar. Cook, stirring often, for 3 to 4 minutes or until apples are lightly caramelized. Scrape apple mixture and syrup into 10-inch round glass baking dish. Reserve.

Meanwhile, in saucepan set over medium heat, heat milk just until bubbles form around edges. Whisking constantly, add some of the milk to eggs; mix until well incorporated; add remaining milk, nutmeg, vanilla, and remaining sugar and mix well. Pour over apple mixture.

Set baking dish inside large roasting pan; pour enough boiling water in roasting pan to come halfway up sides of baking dish. Place in 325°F oven for 45 to 50 minutes or until custard is set but still jiggly. Carefully remove baking dish to cooling rack; sprinkle with walnuts. Cool to room temperature before serving. Makes 6 to 8 servings.

Peaches in Chartreuse Jelly

Mrs. Beeton, the mother of British cuisine, popularized jelly desserts, which, before the advent of instant gelatin, were time-consuming and labor-intensive. Serving a jelly to guests meant that the meal was a special one. This recipe combines the sweetness of peaches poached in sugar syrup with the potent herbal essences of Chartreuse liqueur.

3	large clingstone peaches
4 cups	water
2 cups	granulated sugar
1/4 cup	lemon juice
1	cinnamon stick
3	whole cloves
	Fresh lemon balm leaves or edible flowers

CHARTREUSE JELLY

5 tsp	powdered gelatin
2 cups	water
1/3 cup	granulated sugar
1 cup	Chartreuse

CHARTREUSE JELLY: In small bowl, soften gelatin in 1 cup of the water. In pot, bring remaining water to boil. Add sugar, stirring until dissolved. Remove from heat; add Chartreuse and stir to combine. Pour in softened gelatin, stirring constantly until dissolved. Pour gelatin mixture into 9- x 13-inch glass baking dish lined with waxed paper; refrigerate for 2 hours or until completely set. (If making ahead, cover jelly at this point.)

❧ Meanwhile, immerse peaches in large pot of boiling water for 30 seconds; remove and immediately plunge into cold water. Slip off skins; halve and gently remove stones.

❧ In large pot, combine water and sugar: cook over medium heat, stirring gently, until sugar is dissolved. Bring to boil and cook for 1 minute or until syrup is clear. Add lemon juice, cinnamon stick, and cloves.

❧ Add prepared peaches to hot syrup. Cut a circle of parchment paper slightly smaller than pot; place over top of peaches to insure they remain immersed during cooking (alternatively, use lid from smaller pot to keep fruit submerged).

❧ Bring syrup just to the boil; reduce heat to medium-low and poach peaches gently for 6 minutes or just until soft enough to be easily cut with a spoon. Let cool in syrup. May be stored in syrup in refrigerator for up to 24 hours.

❧ To serve, turn jelly out onto cutting board. Carefully remove waxed paper and roughly chop two-thirds of jelly with knife or edge of large spoon. Divide broken jelly among 6 dessert plates. Using knife or cookie cutter, cut remaining third of jelly into decorative shapes. Using spatula, carefully arrange shapes around outer edge of each bed of jelly.

❧ Slice peaches from one end almost to the other; fan out on bed of jelly. Garnish with lemon balm leaves or edible flowers. Makes 6 servings.

Chocolate Painted Eclairs with French Vanilla Cream

Both the pastry and the filling (standard French pastry cream) date back to the Renaissance, when the Arab art of pastry making invaded Europe by way of Italy. Making perfect choux pastry is a skill acquired through practice. Don't be alarmed if your first attempt tastes better than it looks.

PASTRY CREAM

6	egg yolks
1/2 cup	granulated sugar
5 tbsp	all-purpose flour
2 cups	milk
I	vanilla bean, halved lengthwise
I tbsp	butter
1/2 cup	whipping cream

CHOUX PASTRY

I cup	water
1/2 cup	butter
Pinch	salt
I 1/4 cups	all-purpose flour
5	eggs, room temperature
I tbsp	water
3 oz	bittersweet chocolate
	Icing sugar or edible gold flakes

PASTRY CREAM: In bowl, whisk together egg yolks and 1/4 cup of the sugar for 2 minutes or until pale yellow. Adding flour in 3 additions, stir until well mixed.

❧ In saucepan, heat milk, remaining sugar, and vanilla bean over medium heat, stirring often, for 8 to 10 minutes or until sugar is dissolved and small bubbles are beginning to form around edges of pot. Stirring constantly, pour about one-third of the milk mixture into egg mixture and stir until thoroughly combined. Pour egg mixture into remaining milk and cook, stirring, for 3 to 4 minutes or until mixture begins to bubble. Continue to cook, stirring, for 2 to 3 minutes or until mixture begins to mound and hold its shape; remove from heat. Stir in butter and remove vanilla bean. Transfer to bowl, cover with plastic wrap touching surface of custard, and cool to room temperature.

❧ Beat whipping cream until stiff; add a large dollop of cream to cooled pastry cream and fold in; add remaining whipped cream and fold in until almost combined. Transfer to pastry bag fitted with 1/2-inch star tube. Place in refrigerator until completely chilled.

❧ CHOUX PASTRY: Meanwhile, in heavy-bottomed saucepan set over high heat, bring water, butter, and salt just to boil. Remove from heat and add flour all at once, stirring vigorously with wooden spoon until mixture comes away from sides of pan, making a smooth ball.

❧ Reduce heat to medium-low and cook flour mixture, stirring constantly, for 2 minutes or until coating begins to form on bottom of pan. Turn into large bowl; stir for 30 seconds.

❧ Make well in middle of dough and, using electric mixer, beat in 4 of the eggs, one at a time, beating well after each addition. Continue beating until mixture is smooth and shiny and holds its shape when lifted.

❧ Place dough into piping bag fitted with 3/4-inch wide tip. On parchment-lined baking sheets, pipe fingers of dough about 4 inches long and 1 inch wide. In bowl, beat together remaining egg and I tbsp water; brush each bun lightly, being careful not to drip down sides. Bake in 425°F oven for I2 minutes; reduce heat to 375°F and bake for 5 minutes longer or until golden brown. With sharp knife, pierce side of each éclair twice. Turn oven off and let éclairs stand for 5 minutes, then remove and cool on rack.

🍇 Melt chocolate over barely simmering water. Brush top of each cooled éclair with enough chocolate to coat well. Cool in refrigerator for 5 minutes to harden chocolate.

🍇 Halve éclairs lengthwise. Pull out any sticky dough in center; discard. Pipe pastry cream into bottom of each éclair. Replace chocolate-covered tops. Dust with icing sugar or edible gold flakes just before serving. Makes 25 to 30 small éclairs.

French Vanilla Ice Cream

For this dish it's best to use an automatic ice-cream maker. In the Edwardian era such labor-saving devices existed only in up-to-date commercial kitchens such as the Titanic's, which boasted "electrically-driven triturating, slicing, potato-peeling, mincing, whisking, and freezing machines."

2 cups	light (cereal) cream
I	vanilla bean, halved lengthwise
5	egg yolks
2/3 cup	granulated sugar
I cup	whipping cream

In heavy-bottomed saucepan, combine light cream and vanilla bean over medium heat; heat just until small bubbles start to form around edges of pan. Remove from heat; cover and let stand for I5 minutes.

🍇 Meanwhile, in large bowl, whisk together egg yolks and sugar for I to 2 minutes or until pale and slightly thickened. Remove vanilla bean from pot. Gradually whisk warmed cream into egg mixture.

🍇 Return mixture to saucepan and cook over medium heat, stirring constantly, for 5 minutes or until thick enough to coat back of spoon.

🍇 Remove from heat and blend in whipping cream. Place, uncovered, in refrigerator; cool completely, stirring often.

🍇 Pour mixture into ice-cream maker and freeze following manufacturer's instructions. Or, pour mixture into chilled, shallow metal pan; cover and freeze for 3 hours or until firm. Break up into pieces and transfer to food processor; puree until smooth. Pour into chilled, airtight container; freeze for I hour or until firm. Soften in refrigerator for 20 minutes before serving. Makes 3 1/2 cups and serves 6.

Tips: Especially in summer, pre-chill all containers. Do not boil custard or eggs will "scramble" and ice cream will be ruined. If storing ice cream for more than a few days, reprocess ice cream to return it to its original silken texture.

The denouement of this long and lavish meal came in the form of cheese and fruit. Although neither cheese nor fruit are mentioned on the menu, we know from eyewitnesses that both the first- and second-class dining saloon tables that last evening were adorned with big baskets of fresh fruit, topped with "huge bunches of grapes as large as Damsons" according to one survivor. Cheese would have been their inevitable accompaniment. Among the cheeses the *Titanic* carried were Cheshire, Stilton, Gorgonzola, Edam, Camembert, Roquefort, St. Ivel, and Cheddar.

Jean-Paul Aron has this to say about the last course of an Edwardian meal: "The dessert is defined more by its function than its contents. We have reached the finale: it is the counterpart to the overture. It was the task of the latter to create the right atmosphere; it is for the dessert to soften the blow of departure, that plunge into the void which engulfs the eaters until their next indulgence."

AFTER DINNER

After dessert, the stewards offered coffee, which in France had been a standard after-dinner beverage since about 1860. On board the *Titanic*, coffee was probably made by a drip process, although the much stronger Turkish coffee may well have been available in first class. Either way, coffee was typically accompanied by cigars, port, and liqueurs, then called "cordials." Often the liqueur was poured straight into the coffee, which meant the cups were served only three-quarters full.

The Second-Class Dining Saloon

S ECOND CLASS ON THE *TITANIC* WOULD have been first class on most ships of the day, both in terms of the food served and the atmosphere in which it was consumed. The second-class dining saloon, with its long tables and swivel chairs bolted to the floor, was a comfortable and commodious room, paneled tastefully with oak in an "early English style," according to *The Shipbuilder*. Like the first-class dining saloon, it spanned the entire width of the ship, permitting natural light to enter through the large porthole windows that ran along each side.

The *Titanic*'s spacious, oak-paneled, second-class dining saloon was almost identical to the *Olympic*'s (right). The pattern of the saloon's china service is shown in this cream soup bowl and saucer (left).

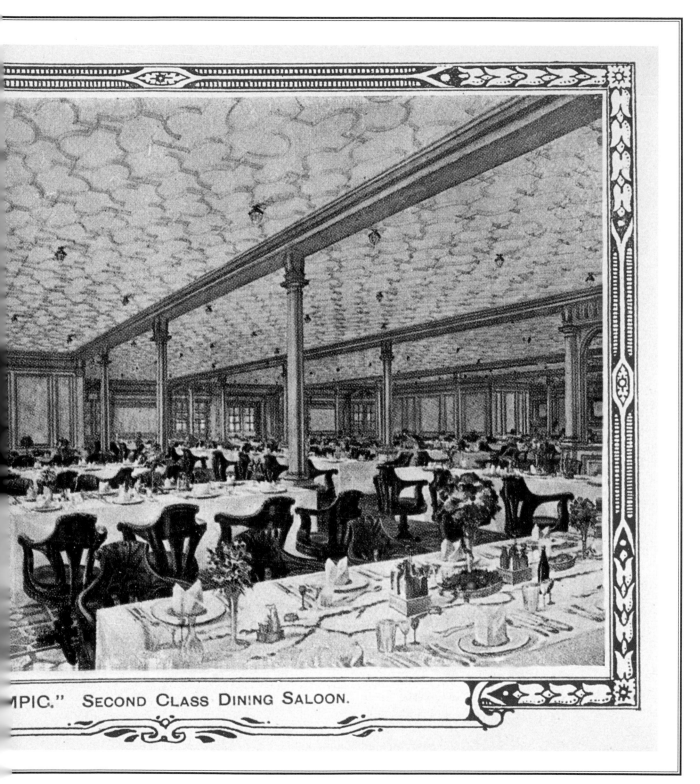

MPIC." SECOND CLASS DINING SALOON.

The Second-Class Dining Saloon

THE FOOD IN SECOND CLASS, THOUGH simpler than in first, was still lavish compared to what most of its middle-class clientele were used to. It also represented a clear marriage of British and American food tastes, plum pudding sharing space with American ice cream. The dishes came from the same galley as first class and were cooked to the highest standard.

One second-class passenger, however, complained later that dinner on the last evening was "too heavy and too rich," but allowed that she enjoyed it nonetheless and commented that "no effort had been spared to give even the second cabin passengers . . . the best dinner that money could buy." Certainly no one went hungry after this solid, three-course meal, far closer to a family Sunday dinner than to the champagne-and-caviar gourmandry of the elegant "Ritz" restaurant two decks above.

In all probability, this meal was served very much like a meal ordered in a modern restaurant. After the soup, diners would have chosen one main course, which would have arrived at the table on a single plate garnished with potatoes or rice and vegetables.

A 1920s photograph of second-class dining aboard R.M.S. *Olympic* (left) shows that the long rows of tables (seen on previous page) have given way to more casual seating. (Above) The *Titanic*'s second-class menu for April 14, 1912.

FIRST COURSE — SOUP
Consommé with Tapioca

SECOND COURSE — MAIN DISHES
Baked Haddock with Sharp Sauce
Curried Chicken and Rice
Lamb with Mint Sauce (recipe page 79)
Roast Turkey with Savory Cranberry Sauce
Turnip Puree
Green Peas
Boiled Rice
Boiled and Roast Potatoes

THIRD COURSE — DESSERTS
Plum Pudding with Sweet Sauce
Wine Jelly
Coconut Sandwich
American Ice Cream
Assorted Nuts
Fresh Fruit
Cheese, Biscuits

AFTER DINNER
Coffee

Consommé with Tapioca

This pleasing starter is made from the same savory beef consommé that formed the base of consommé Olga in first class. The fashion of serving firm tapioca pudding in shimmering bowls of clarified broth has given way to the better-known custom of floating decoratively cut pieces of Royale custard or noodles in a clear soup.

6 cups	clarified consommé (see page 73)
	GARNISH
2	egg yolks
1/2 cup	milk
1/4 tsp	each salt and pepper
1 tbsp	quick-cooking tapioca
2 tbsp	finely chopped fresh parsley

GARNISH: In small pot, whisk together egg yolks, milk, salt, and pepper. Stir in tapioca and let stand for 5 minutes. Cook tapioca mixture over medium-high heat for 3 to 5 minutes or until mixture thickens enough to hold its shape. Stir in parsley and spread onto greased baking sheet; chill.

🍇 Cut tapioca garnish into decorative shapes using aspic cutters or sharp knife. Carefully place in consommé. Serve immediately. Makes 6 servings.

Tip: Sprinkle with finely chopped parsley for additional garnish if desired.

No recipes have been provided for several items that accompany the main course. The green peas were probably served with butter, salt, and pepper; the boiled rice, as in first class, would likely have been long-grain white rice; and the boiled and roast potatoes presented simply with butter.

Baked Haddock with Sharp Sauce

Haddock was then a staple of British cuisine, served at breakfast (often in its smoked form) and high tea as well as at dinner.

³/4 cup	mayonnaise
I ¹/2 tsp	Dijon mustard
6	skinless haddock fillets (8 oz each)
³/4 cup	fresh bread crumbs
3 tbsp	chopped fresh parsley
3 tbsp	freshly grated Parmesan cheese
I ¹/2 tbsp	chopped fresh chives
	Lemon wedges
	SHARP SAUCE
2 tbsp	butter
I	small onion, finely chopped
I tbsp	brown sugar
¹/4 tsp	each salt and pepper
I tbsp	all-purpose flour
³/4 cup	water
2 tbsp	tomato paste
I tbsp	cider vinegar
I tsp	dry mustard
I tsp	Worcestershire sauce
Dash	hot pepper sauce

SHARP SAUCE: In small saucepan, melt butter over medium heat; add onion and cook, stirring often, for 5 minutes or until softened. Increase heat to medium-high and stir in brown sugar, salt, and pepper; continue to cook, stirring frequently, for 5 minutes longer or until onions are well browned. Sprinkle with flour and cook, stirring, for 45 seconds. Stir in water, tomato paste, vinegar, dry mustard, Worcestershire sauce, and hot pepper sauce. Bring to boil and reduce heat to low. Simmer for 2 minutes or until thickened. Strain and keep warm.

In small dish, combine mayonnaise and mustard. Place fillets on greased baking sheet. Using back of spoon, spread mayonnaise mixture evenly over top of fish. Stir together bread crumbs, parsley, and Parmesan; sprinkle over fillets.

Place fish in 400°F oven for 7 to 8 minutes or until fish is opaque and flakes easily with fork. Broil for I to 2 minutes or until topping is evenly browned. Transfer to heated platter and sprinkle with chives; serve with lemon wedges and sharp sauce on the side. Makes 6 servings.

Curried Chicken and Rice

The English had learned to love the flavor of curry during the many years that India was the brightest jewel in the imperial crown.

I	chicken (3 ¹/₂ lb)
I	lime
3 tbsp	freshly minced ginger
I	clove garlic, minced
2 tbsp	oil
2 tbsp	mild curry powder
I	onion, chopped
I tbsp	liquid honey
I ¹/₃ cups	long-grain rice
2 ¹/₂ cups	water
¹/₂ tsp	salt
¹/₄ cup	sultana (golden) raisins
¹/₄ cup	chopped green onion or fresh chives
	Chutney

Using fingers, remove skin from chicken; pat dry and cut into equal-sized pieces. Discard back.

🍇 Using zester, remove zest from lime and chop finely; juice lime. In bowl, combine lime zest, lime juice, ginger, and garlic; add chicken, turning to coat well. Let stand for 30 minutes.

🍇 In large, deep, non-stick skillet, heat I tbsp of the oil over medium-high heat. Add chicken pieces and marinade; cook for 10 minutes or until well colored on all sides. Remove chicken from pan; reduce heat to medium and stir in remaining oil and curry powder; cook, stirring often, for 3 minutes. Stir in onion and honey; continue to cook, stirring occasionally, for 3 minutes. Stir in rice and cook for 3 minutes or until rice is slightly browned; stir in water, salt, and raisins.

🍇 Nestle chicken into rice. Bring to boil; cover with tight-fitting lid and reduce heat to low. Simmer for 25 to 30 minutes or until juices run clear when chicken thigh is pierced. Transfer to heated platter; garnish with green onions. Serve with chutney. Makes 6 servings.

Savory Cranberry Sauce

I tbsp	vegetable oil
I	small onion, finely chopped
I	clove garlic, minced
¹/₄ cup	port
2 tbsp	balsamic vinegar
I ¹/₂ cups	cranberries, fresh or frozen (thawed)
¹/₂ cup	granulated sugar
¹/₄ tsp	each salt and pepper

In small saucepan, heat oil over medium heat; stir in onion and garlic and cook, stirring occasionally, for 5 minutes or until softened. Stir in port and balsamic vinegar; boil for 5 minutes or until reduced to about 3 tbsp.

🍇 Meanwhile, slice cranberries in half; in bowl, stir together cranberries, sugar, salt, and pepper. Mix into onion mixture; bring to boil and cook, stirring often, for 8 to 10 minutes or until cranberries are tender and sauce is thick.

🍇 Transfer to non-metallic container; store in refrigerator, tightly covered, for up to I week or in freezer for up to I month. Makes I cup.

Roast Turkey with Savory Cranberry Sauce

By the turn of the century, the North American turkey had become familiar British fare,
replacing the traditional goose at many an English Christmas table. Here it is presented in classic American
style with bread stuffing and accompanied by cranberry sauce, which at this period was
more like a sauce than a preserve.

1	turkey (10 lb)
2 tbsp	butter, softened
1 tsp	crumbled sage leaves
1/2 tsp	each salt and pepper

STUFFING

2 tbsp	butter
2	onions, chopped
1 cup	finely chopped celery
1 tsp	each crumbled sage, thyme, and marjoram leaves
3/4 tsp	each salt and pepper
1/2 cup	sherry
10 cups	cubed bread, lightly toasted
1/2 cup	chopped fresh parsley
1/4 cup	chicken stock

GRAVY

3 cups	chicken stock
1	onion, chopped
1	bay leaf
2 tbsp	all-purpose flour
	Salt and pepper
	SAVORY CRANBERRY SAUCE (recipe opposite page)

STUFFING: In skillet, melt butter over medium heat. Stir in onions, celery, sage, thyme, marjoram, salt, and pepper; cook, stirring occasionally, for 10 minutes or until browned. Stir in sherry; bring to boil. Boil for 5 minutes or until liquid is almost completely evaporated. Cool slightly. Gently stir in bread and parsley; drizzle over chicken stock, stirring to combine. Reserve.

❦ Remove giblets and neck from turkey cavity; reserve for gravy. Rinse turkey inside and out with running water. Pat dry. Stir together butter, sage, salt, and pepper; rub over turkey, inside and out. Loosely pack stuffing into neck and body cavities, fold over and skewer neck flap closed over stuffing. Tie legs together. Bend wing tips underneath bird.

❦ Place turkey, breast side up, on rack in roasting pan. Tent with foil and roast in 325°F oven for about 1 1/2 hours, basting with pan juices every 30 minutes. Remove foil and continue to roast for 1 3/4 hours, basting every half hour, or until instant-read meat thermometer inserted into thickest part of thigh reads 185°F. Let rest for 20 minutes before carving.

❦ GRAVY: Meanwhile, in saucepan, bring chicken stock, turkey neck, giblets, onion, and bay leaf to boil; reduce heat and simmer, covered, for 1 hour; strain, reserving liquid. While cooked turkey rests, skim excess fat from roasting pan. Set pan over high heat; whisk in flour until well combined. Gradually whisk in reserved giblet stock. Bring to boil and cook, stirring constantly, for 2 minutes or until thickened. Season to taste with salt and pepper. Strain and serve alongside turkey. Makes 6 servings.

Turnip Puree

More popular in Britain and on the Continent than in North America, turnips make a lovely puree,
here rendered slightly exotic by the addition of cardamom.

2 lb	turnips
2 tbsp	butter
2 tbsp	honey
1/4 tsp	ground cardamom
1/2 cup	milk, heated
1/2 tsp	each salt and pepper

Peel turnips and cut into chunks; place in large saucepan. Cover with cold salted water and bring to boil; reduce heat and simmer for 25 to 30 minutes or until fork-tender.

Drain well and transfer to food processor; add butter, honey, and cardamom; process until smooth. With motor running, gradually pour in heated milk, salt, and pepper. Continue to process until turnips are light and creamy. Makes 6 servings.

THIRD COURSE — DESSERTS

Dessert in second class included a hot and cold sweet, ice cream, assorted nuts, fresh fruit, cheese, and coffee. The assorted nuts may actually have been a mixture of shelled nuts and dried fruits. The fresh fruit was undoubtedly a large bowl of the fruit that so impressed the first- and second-class passengers. "Cheese biscuits" simply means assorted cheeses served with biscuits or crackers.

Sweet Sauce

1/4 cup	butter, softened
1/2 cup	granulated sugar
1	egg
1/2 cup	sherry or orange juice
1 tbsp	grated orange rind
1 tsp	vanilla

In top of double boiler or heatproof bowl, beat together butter and sugar until light and fluffy. Add egg, beating constantly, until well combined. Stir in sherry and orange rind until smooth. Place over barely simmering water and cook, stirring constantly, for 10 to 12 minutes or until thick enough to coat back of spoon. Remove from heat and add vanilla. Serve warm. Makes 1 1/2 cups and is sufficient for 12 servings of pudding.

Plum Pudding with Sweet Sauce

*Given the time and effort that goes into plum pudding—which originated in Britain about two hundred years ago—
passengers must have regarded this dessert item as a particularly festive treat. Ironically, plums
(in the form of dried prunes) have completely disappeared from this archetypal British delicacy, but would certainly
have been part of the dish consumed at the last dinner.*

I cup	chopped suet
I ½ cups	each slivered blanched almonds, raisins, currants, and candied peel
¼ cup	pitted, chopped prunes
I ½ cups	all-purpose flour
I cup	dry bread crumbs
I tsp	each cinnamon and nutmeg
½ tsp	allspice
½ cup	butter, softened
⅔ cup	granulated sugar
5	eggs, beaten
½ cup	milk
⅓ cup	rum or orange juice

SWEET SAUCE
(recipe opposite page)

In large bowl, stir together suet, almonds, raisins, currants, candied peel, prunes, flour, bread crumbs, cinnamon, nutmeg, and allspice.

❧ In another bowl, beat together butter and sugar. Add eggs, one at a time, beating well after each addition. Stir in milk and rum. Using large spoon, stir half of the fruit mixture into the egg mixture until well combined. Stir in remaining fruit mixture.

❧ Grease and flour a 6-cup (1.5 L) pudding mold. Spoon in pudding mixture, packing lightly. Cover with lid.

❧ Place mold in rack of steamer or on rack in large pot; pour in enough boiling water to come two-thirds of the way up sides of mold. Cover and simmer on low heat, adding more boiling water as necessary, for 2 ½ to 3 hours or until tester inserted in center comes out clean.

❧ Unmold pudding onto serving dish and serve with sweet sauce. Makes 12 to 15 servings.

American Ice Cream

At the time of the Titanic's maiden voyage, ice cream was extremely popular in both France and the United States. In France, egg yolks were added to make the mixture both richer and smoother. The American style, without any eggs, was popularized by Dolly Madison after her husband became president in 1809.

²/₃ cup	granulated sugar
¹/₃ cup	lemon juice
Pinch	salt
2 cups	light (cereal) cream
2 tbsp	finely chopped grated lemon zest
1 cup	whipping cream

In small pot or microwave-proof dish, combine sugar, lemon juice, and salt; heat over medium heat until sugar is dissolved. Meanwhile, in heavy-bottomed saucepan, combine light cream with lemon zest; heat over medium heat for 6 to 8 minutes just until small bubbles start to form around edges of pot. Remove from heat.

❧ Whisk sugar mixture and whipping cream into lemon zest mixture until smooth. Place in refrigerator uncovered; cool completely, stirring often.

❧ Pour mixture into ice-cream maker and proceed following manufacturer's instructions. Or, pour mixture into chilled, shallow metal pan; cover and freeze for about 3 hours or until firm. Break up into pieces and transfer to food processor; puree until smooth. Pour into chilled airtight container; freeze for 1 hour or until firm. Soften in refrigerator for 20 minutes before serving. Makes 3 cups and serves 6.

Tip If working in a warm environment, pre-chill all containers.

The Third-Class Dining Saloon

ALTHOUGH SPARTAN, THE THIRD-CLASS dining room located amidships on F-deck was a vast improvement over the dining facilities steerage passengers had come to expect. White Star realized that for all the glitter of first class, the bread and butter of its transatlantic run

would be the many thousands of working-class Europeans wanting to emigrate to the rapidly expanding economies of North America.

Actually, there were two third-class dining rooms, the allotted space being bisected by one of the ship's watertight bulkheads. In each, the white-enameled walls were enlivened by colorful framed White Star posters, and the tables were set with linen tablecloths and waited on by stewards. Third class had its own kitchen, where the hearty, nourishing meals were prepared.

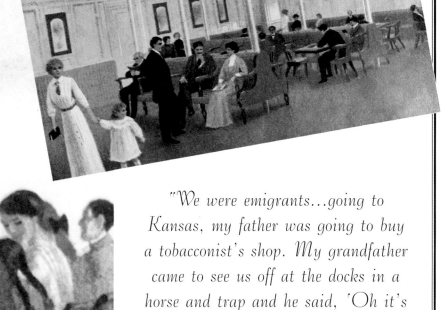

"We were emigrants...going to Kansas, my father was going to buy a tobacconist's shop. My grandfather came to see us off at the docks in a horse and trap and he said, 'Oh it's a wonderful ship. You'll have a wonderful time.'"

— Third-class passenger Millvina Dean

Illustrations in a White Star brochure depict the third-class dining saloon (left) and general room (above). Third class had come a long way from the days when steerage passengers were required to bring their own food and cutlery.

The Third-Class Dining Saloon

I N THIRD CLASS, THE MAIN SUNDAY MEAL WAS MIDDAY DINNER. The traditional English savory tea, served in the late afternoon was the last meal of the day. One writer of the period, looking down his long nose at his inferiors, described an English working class tea as "the most eccentric of meals, and one of the greatest injuries a gourmet could possibly conceive. . . . This incongruous kind of food may, no doubt, be quite nice and tasty for this class of people, but it must shock any one endowed with refined epicurean instinct." On the *Titanic*, however, the third-class tea looks quite palatable. And for those requiring additional sustenance before bed, a light supper of cabin biscuits and cheese, followed by gruel and coffee, finished off the day.

WHITE STAR LINE
Specimen Third Class Bill of Fare
Subject to Alteration as Circumstances Require

	Sunday	Monday	Tuesday	Wednesday	Thursday	Friday	Saturday
Breakfast	Quaker Oats and Milk Smoked Herrings and Jacket Potatoes Boiled Eggs Fresh Bread and Butter Marmalade, Swedish Bread Tea and Coffee	Oatmeal Porridge and Milk Irish Stew Broiled Sausages Fresh Bread and Butter Marmalade, Swedish Bread Tea and Coffee	Oatmeal Porridge and Milk Ling Fish, Egg Sauce Fried Tripe and Onions Jacket Potatoes Fresh Bread and Butter Marmalade, Swedish Bread Tea and Coffee	Quaker Oats and Milk Smoked Herrings Beefsteak and Onions Jacket Potatoes Fresh Bread and Butter Marmalade, Swedish Bread Tea and Coffee	Oatmeal Porridge and Milk Liver and Bacon Irish Stew Fresh Bread and Butter Marmalade, Swedish Bread Tea and Coffee	Quaker Oats and Milk Smoked Herrings Jacket Potatoes Curried Beef and Rice Fresh Bread and Butter Marmalade, Swedish Bread Tea and Coffee	Oatmeal Porridge and Milk Vegetable Stew Fried Tripe and Onions Fresh Bread and Butter Marmalade, Swedish Bread Tea and Coffee
Dinner ..	Vegetable Soup Roast Pork, Sage and Onions Green Peas Boiled Potatoes Cabin Biscuits, Fresh Bread Plum Pudding, Sweet Sauce Oranges	Barley Broth Beefsteak and Kidney Pie Carrots and Turnips Boiled Potatoes Cabin Biscuits, Fresh Bread Stewed Apples and Rice	Pea Soup Fricassee Rabbit and Bacon Lima Beans, Boiled Potatoes Cabin Biscuits, Fresh Bread Semolina Pudding Apples	Rice Soup Corned Beef and Cabbage Boiled Potatoes Cabin Biscuits, Fresh Bread Peaches and Rice	Vegetable Soup Boiled Mutton and Caper Sauce Green Peas, Boiled Potatoes Cabin Biscuits, Fresh Bread Plum Pudding, Sweet Sauce	Pea Soup Ling Fish, Egg Salad Cold Beef and Pickles Cabbage, Boiled Potatoes Cabin Biscuits, Fresh Bread Cornaline Pudding Oranges	Bouillon Soup Roast Beef and Brown Gravy Green Beans, Boiled Potatoes Cabin Biscuits, Fresh Bread Prunes and Rice
Tea	Ragout of Beef, Potatoes and Pickles Apricots Fresh Bread and Butter Currant Buns Tea	Curried Mutton and Rice Cheese and Pickles Fresh Bread and Butter Damson Jam Swedish Bread Tea	Haricot Mutton Pickles Prunes and Rice Fresh Bread and Butter Swedish Bread	Brawn Cheese and Pickles Fresh Bread and Butter Rhubarb Jam Currant Buns Tea	Sausage and Mashed Potatoes Dry Hash Apples and Rice Fresh Bread and Butter Swedish Bread Tea	Cod Fish Cakes Cheese and Pickles Fresh Bread and Butter Plum and Apple Jam Swedish Bread Tea	Rabbit Pie Baked Potatoes Fresh Bread and Butter Rhubarb and Ginger Jam Swedish Bread, Tea

SUPPER—Every Day.—Cabin Biscuits and Cheese.   Gruel, Coffee.   Fresh Fish served as substitute for Salt Fish as opportunity offers

Kosher Meat Supplied and Cooked for Jewish Passengers as desired

A typical White Star bill of fare (above) shows that the main meal in the third-class dining saloon (right) was served in the middle of the day.

This water-stained menu from April 12 (right) was recovered from the body of a third-class passenger. The third-class table ticket (below), printed in Swedish, German, and Finnish as well as English, admitted the bearer to the first of two seatings for each meal.

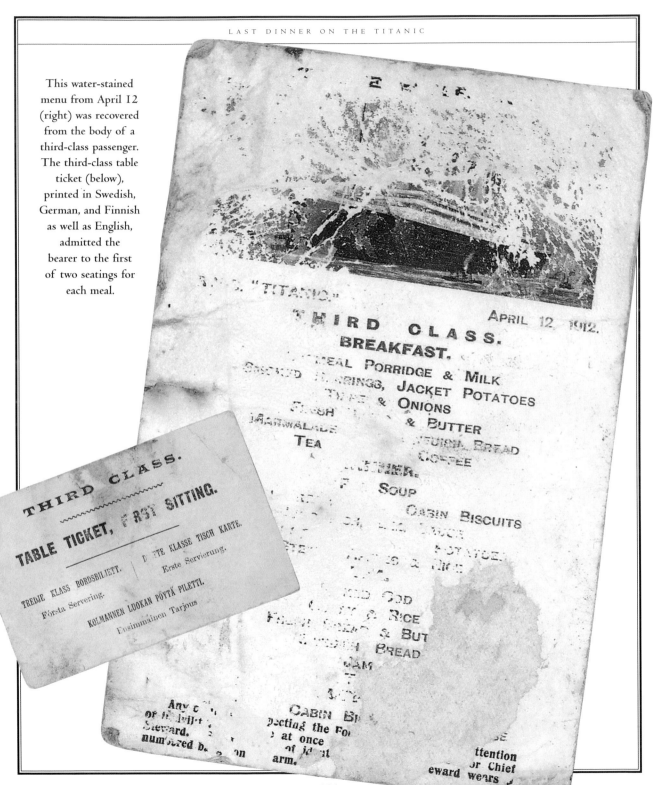

R.M.S. "TITANIC"

THIRD CLASS.
BREAKFAST.

APRIL 12, 1912.

OATMEAL PORRIDGE & MILK
SMOKED HERRINGS, JACKET POTATOES
TRIPE & ONIONS
FRESH & BUTTER
MARMALADE SWEDISH BREAD
TEA COFFEE

DINNER.

SOUP
CABIN BISCUITS
POTATOES
& RICE
COD
& RICE
& BUTTER
SWEDISH BREAD
JAM

CABIN BI

THIRD CLASS.

TABLE TICKET, FIRST SITTING.

TREDJE KLASS BORDSBILJETT.
Första Servering.

DRITTE KLASSE TISCH KARTE.
Erste Servierung.

KOLMANNEN LUOKAN PÖYTÄ PILETTI.
Ensimmäinen Tarjous.

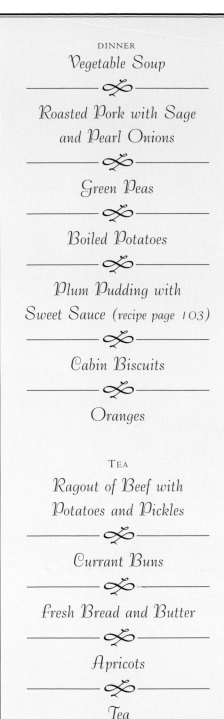

DINNER

Vegetable Soup

꘎

Roasted Pork with Sage
and Pearl Onions

꘎

Green Peas

꘎

Boiled Potatoes

꘎

Plum Pudding with
Sweet Sauce (recipe page 103)

꘎

Cabin Biscuits

꘎

Oranges

TEA

Ragout of Beef with
Potatoes and Pickles

꘎

Currant Buns

꘎

Fresh Bread and Butter

꘎

Apricots

꘎

Tea

Vegetable Soup

*Unlike the ritzier soups served in the two upper-class saloons,
this soup is rustic and easy to prepare.*

2 tbsp	butter
I	finely chopped onion
I cup	each sliced celery and carrot
I	potato, peeled and cubed
5	cloves garlic, minced
I tsp	each dried oregano and thyme
I	bay leaf
6 cups	chicken or vegetable stock
2 cups	white kidney beans, drained
I cup	corn kernels
I cup	asparagus tips
2 cups	shredded Swiss chard or spinach
	Salt and pepper

In large pot, melt butter over medium heat. Stir in onion, celery, carrot, potato, garlic, oregano, thyme, and bay leaf. Cover and cook, stirring often, for 10 minutes or until onion is translucent.

꘎ Stir in stock and bring to boil. Reduce heat to medium and simmer for 15 to 20 minutes or until vegetables are almost tender.

꘎ Meanwhile, drain and rinse beans. Stir beans, corn, and asparagus into vegetable mixture. Cook for 5 minutes or until asparagus is bright green and tender. Stir in Swiss chard and season to taste with salt and pepper. Makes 6 servings.

Roasted Pork with Sage and Pearl Onions

Today cooks serve pork roasts that are still slightly pink, but at the beginning of the century,
anything but well done pork posed a health hazard. Since pork becomes tough when well done,
the custom was to marinate the meat overnight to increase its moisture content and improve its taste.
This recipe combines the best of both ages: the meat is cooked to the modern standard of doneness,
but marinated to maximize juiciness and flavor.

1	onion, finely chopped
3	cloves garlic, minced
1/4 cup	vegetable oil
1/4 cup	port
1/4 cup	chopped fresh sage (or 2 tbsp dry, crumbled sage leaves)
1/2 tsp	pepper
1	boneless pork shoulder butt, rolled and tied (3 lb)
1 1/2 cups	small button mushrooms
1 tsp	butter
3 cups	chicken stock
1 1/2 cups	pearl onions
1 tbsp	all-purpose flour
1/2 cup	port
	Salt and pepper

Place onion, garlic, vegetable oil, port, sage, and pepper in food processor. Blend until onion and sage are almost smooth. Place pork roast in large, shallow bowl; pour sage mixture over pork, turning to coat. Cover and refrigerate for 24 hours, turning occasionally.

❦ Remove roast from refrigerator and let come to room temperature for 30 minutes. Meanwhile, clean mushrooms and remove stems; reserve stems for another use.

❦ In large skillet, melt butter over medium-high heat. Brown pork on all sides. Place in bottom of roasting pan with marinating juices. Pour 1/2 cup of the chicken stock over pork and surround with pearl onions. Bake in 325°F oven for 1 hour; add mushrooms and another 1/2 cup of the chicken stock to pan. Continue to cook for about 60 minutes or until instant-read meat thermometer registers 160°F or until juices run clear and meat is just barely pink in center. Remove roast and vegetables from pan; tent with foil and let stand for 15 minutes.

❦ Meanwhile, set roasting pan over medium heat; sprinkle flour into pan; cook, stirring, for 1 minute. Pour in remaining stock and port; bring to boil and cook for 3 minutes or until thickened. Strain. Season with salt and pepper to taste.

❦ Slice roast and arrange on platter. Spoon sauce over pork slices and serve pork surrounded with onions and mushroom caps. Makes 6 servings.

Cabin Biscuits

More like crackers than biscuits, these simple breads were a shipboard remedy
for unsettled stomachs. In their original form, they were fairly unpalatable. Here we offer some suggestions
for making them more of a snack and less of a medicine.

2 cups all-purpose
flour

¹/₂ tsp salt

1 tsp shortening

³/₄ cup water

In bowl, mix together flour and salt. Using fingertips, work shortening into flour until mixture resembles fine crumbs. Make well in dry ingredients and pour in water. Blend until mixture forms a stiff dough, adding up to 2 tsp extra water if necessary.

❧ Place on lightly floured surface and roll into cylinder. Cut into 25 evenly sized pieces; loosely cover with plastic wrap; let rest for 15 minutes. Roll each piece of dough into 2 ¹/₂-inch circle. Prick all over with fork. Place on ungreased baking sheet; bake in 375°F oven for about 15 minutes or until lightly browned. Makes 25 biscuits.

Variations:

❧ Spray unbaked biscuits lightly with water and sprinkle with rock salt. Bake as above.

❧ After 10 minutes of baking, sprinkle biscuits with Parmesan cheese and chopped fresh parsley; bake for 5 minutes longer.

❧ Before baking, brush unbaked biscuits lightly with butter; sprinkle with cinnamon and sugar.

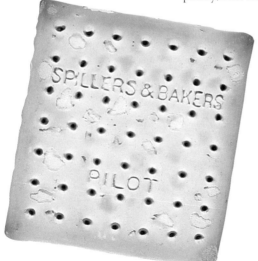

A hardtack biscuit saved from one
of the *Titanic*'s lifeboats.

"The tea of the English
working-class is the most eccentric
of meals, and one of the greatest
injuries a gourmet could possibly
conceive...it must shock anyone endowed
with refined epicurean instinct."

— J. Rey in *The Whole Art of Dining*, 1914

In addition to the recipes given here, a typical *Titanic* tea included fresh bread and butter, apricots, and, of course, tea.

Ragout of Beef with Potatoes and Pickles

The word ragout *dates back to 1642, when it meant anything that stimulates the appetite.*
Gradually it came to mean a stew of regular-sized pieces of meat cooked in a liquid. In this ragoût a l'Anglaise,
or "white ragout," the meat is not browned and the liquid thickened only by cooking potatoes with the meat.
Pickled red cabbage makes a perfect—and traditional—accompaniment.

2	slices bacon, chopped
2	onions, chopped
2	carrots, chopped
2	cloves garlic, minced
2 tsp	dried thyme
1/2 tsp	ground allspice
1/4 tsp	ground nutmeg
6	medium potatoes
2 lb	stewing beef
1 cup	each beef stock and tomato juice
1 tsp	salt
1/2 tsp	pepper
1 tbsp	cider vinegar
1 1/2 cups	tiny peas, fresh or frozen
	Pickled red cabbage

In Dutch oven, cook bacon over medium heat, stirring often, for about 5 minutes or until browned; drain off excess fat and add onions, carrots, garlic, thyme, allspice, and nutmeg to pot. Cook, stirring often, for about 5 minutes or until onions are softened.

❦ Meanwhile, peel and finely dice half of the potatoes. Add to vegetable mixture and cook, stirring occasionally, for 5 minutes. Pat beef dry; stir into vegetable mixture. Stir in beef stock, tomato juice, salt, and pepper; bring to boil. Cover and reduce heat to low; simmer for 1 1/2 hours, stirring occasionally.

❦ Meanwhile, peel remaining potatoes and cut into bite-size pieces. Add to pot; cook, covered, for 15 minutes. Uncover and cook, stirring often, for 15 minutes or until meat is tender and sauce is slightly thickened. Stir in vinegar and peas; cook until peas are heated through. Adjust seasoning to taste. Serve with pickled red cabbage on the side. Makes 6 servings.

Currant Buns

A staple of an English tea, these buns would have pleased the palates of the many British emigrants traveling in third class.

¹/4 cup	lukewarm water
¹/2 cup	granulated sugar
I	pkg active dry yeast (I tbsp)
3 ¹/2 cups	all-purpose flour
¹/2 tsp	salt
³/4 cup	warm milk
¹/4 cup	butter, melted
2	eggs
¹/2 cup	currants
2 tbsp	icing sugar
I tbsp	water

In small bowl or measuring cup, combine warm water and I tbsp of the sugar; sprinkle yeast over top. Let stand for I0 minutes or until frothy.

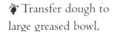 Meanwhile, in large bowl, blend together remaining sugar, flour, and salt. In small bowl, whisk together milk, butter, and eggs. Stir in yeast mixture until combined.

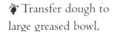 Make well in dry ingredients; using wooden spoon, stir in yeast mixture until soft dough forms. Turn out onto lightly floured board. Knead for 8 minutes or until dough is smooth and elastic.

Another view of the third-class dining saloon.

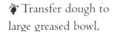 Transfer dough to large greased bowl, turning to coat. Cover with plastic wrap and let rest in a warm place for I hour or until doubled in bulk. Punch down; turn out onto floured surface; knead in currants. Shape into a I2-inch long log. Cut dough into I2 equal pieces.

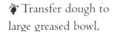 Roll pieces of dough into smooth, seamless balls. Place buns on greased baking sheet leaving about 2 inches between each bun. Cover loosely and let rest for 30 minutes.

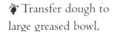 Bake in 400°F oven for I5 minutes or until golden brown. Stir together icing sugar and water; brush over warm buns; let cool on rack. Makes I2 buns.

Conversion Charts

Volume Equivalents

NORTH AMERICAN	METRIC	IMPERIAL
1/4 tsp	1 mL	
1/2 tsp	2 mL	
1 tsp	5 mL	
1 1/2 tsp	7 mL	
1/2 tbsp	7 mL	
1 tbsp	15 mL	
2 tbsp	30 mL	
1/4 cup	60 mL	2 fl oz
1/3 cup	75 mL	2 1/2 fl oz
1/2 cup	125 mL	4 fl oz
2/3 cup	150 mL	5 fl oz (1/4 pint)
3/4 cup	175 mL	6 fl oz
1 cup	250 mL	8 fl oz
1 1/4 cups	300 mL	10 fl oz
1 1/2 cups	375 mL	12 fl oz
2 cups	500 mL	16 fl oz
3 cups	750 mL	24 fl oz
4 cups	1 L	1 3/4 pints
5 cups	1.25 L	2 1/2 pints
6 cups	1.50 L	3 pints
7 cups	1.75 L	3 1/2 pints

Oven Temperature Equivalents

	IMPERIAL	METRIC	GAS MARK
Very Cool	250°F	120°C	1/2
Cool	275°F	140°C	1
Cool	300°F	150°C	2
Warm	325°F	160°C	3
Moderate	350°F	180°C	4
Medium Hot	375°F	190°C	5
Fairly Hot	400°F	200°C	6
Hot	425°F	220°C	7
Very Hot	450°F	230°C	8
Very Hot	475°F	240°C	9

Weight Conversion

INGREDIENT	VOLUME	WEIGHT
Almonds, slivered	1/4 cup/50 mL	1 oz/30 g
	1 1/2 cups/375 mL	6 1/2 oz/180 g
Asparagus tips	1 cup/250 mL	3 1/2 oz/100 g
Barley, pearl	1 cup/250 mL	7 oz/200 g
Basil, chopped fresh	1/4 cup/50 mL	1/2 oz/15 g
Bread, crumbs	1/4 cup/50 mL	2/3 oz/20 g
	1/2 cup/125 mL	1 1/2 oz/40 g
	3/4 cup/175 mL	20 oz/60 g
	1 cup/250 mL	2 1/2 oz/70 g
Bread, cubed	10 cups/2.5 L	18 oz/500 g
Butter	1/4 cup/50 mL	2 oz/50 g
	1/2 cup/125 mL	4 1/2 oz/125 g
	2/3 cup/150 mL	5 oz/150 g
	3/4 cup/175 mL	6 1/2 oz/190 g
Candied peel, chopped	1 1/2 cups/375 mL	11 oz/300 g
Carrot, sliced	1 cup/250 mL	5 oz/150 g
Celery, sliced	1 cup/250 mL	5 oz/150 g
Cherries, pitted	1/2 cup/125 mL	4 1/2 oz/125 g
Coconut, shredded	2/3 cup/150 mL	2 oz/50 g
Corn, kernels	1 cup/250 mL	2 1/2 oz/75 g
Cranberries	1 1/2 cups/375 mL	5 oz/150 g
Currants	1/2 cup/125 mL	2 oz/50 g
	1 1/2 cups/375 mL	6 1/2 oz/190 g
Currants, red	1/2 cup/125 mL	2 1/2 oz/75 g

Ingredient	Volume	Weight
Flour, all-purpose	1/3 cup/75 mL	2 oz/50 g
	1 cup/250 mL	4 1/2 oz/130 g
	1 1/4 cups/300 mL	6 oz/175 g
	1 1/2 cups/375 mL	7 1/2 oz/210 g
	2 cups/500 mL	9 oz/260 g
	3 1/2 cups/875 mL	18 oz/520 g
Grapes, seedless	1/2 cup/125 mL	2 1/2 oz/75 g
Kidney beans	2 cups/500 mL	11 oz/300 g
Mint leaves, lightly packed	1/4 cup/50 mL	1/3 oz/10 g
Mint, fresh, chopped	1/4 cup/50 mL	1/3 oz/10 g
Morels, dried	1/2 cup/125 mL	9 oz/250 g
Mushrooms	1 1/2 cups/375 mL	4 oz/120 g
	2 1/2 cups/625 mL	10 1/2 oz/300 g
Nectarines, thinly sliced	1 cup/250 mL	7 oz/200 g
Onions, green, chopped	1/4 cup/50 mL	1/3 oz/10 g
Onions, pearl	1 1/2 cups/375 mL	6 oz/90 g
Onions, red, finely chopped	1 cup/250 mL	4 oz/120 g
Orange segments	1/2 cup/125 mL	2 1/2 oz/75 g
Parmesan cheese, grated	1/4 cup/50 mL	1 oz/30 g
Parsley, fresh, chopped	1/2 cup/125 mL	2 oz/60 g
Parsley, stems	1/4 cup/50 mL	1/3 oz/10 g
Peas, fresh or frozen	1 1/2 cups/375 mL	8 oz/225 g
	2 cups/500 mL	9 oz/250 g
	4 cups/1 L	18 oz/500 g
Prunes, pitted and chopped	1/4 cup/50 mL	2 oz/50 g
Raisins	1 1/2 cups/375 mL	8 oz/225 g

Ingredient	Volume	Weight
Raisins, sultana (golden)	1/4 cup/50 mL	1 1/2 oz/40 g
	1/2 cup/125 mL	3 oz/75 g
	1 1/2 cups/375 mL	9 oz/225 g
Raspberries	1/2 cup/125 mL	2 1/2 oz/75 g
Rice, cooked	2/3 cup/150 mL	4 1/2 oz/130 g
Rice, long-grain	1 1/3 cups/325 mL	9 1/2 oz/270 g
Romaine lettuce, shredded	1 cup/250 mL	3 oz/75 g
Sage, fresh, chopped	1/4 cup/50 mL	1/3 oz/10 g
Salt pork, chopped	1/4 cup/50 mL	2 oz/50 g
Suet, chopped	1 cup/250 mL	4 1/2 oz/125 g
Sugar, brown	1/2 cup/125 mL	3 oz/75 g
Sugar, fruit	1/2 cup/125 mL	3 1/2 oz/90 g
Sugar, granulated	1/4 cup/50 mL	2 oz/50 g
	1/3 cup/75 mL	2 1/2 oz/70 g
	1/2 cup/125 mL	3 1/2 oz/90 g
	2/3 cup/150 mL	4 oz/120 g
	2 cups/500 mL	13 oz/375 g
Sugar, icing	3/4 cup/175 mL	3 1/2 oz/90 g
Swiss chard, shredded	2 cups/500 mL	3 1/2 oz/90 g
Turnips	6 cups/1.5 L	2 lb/1 kg
Walnuts, toasted	1/4 cup/50 mL	2 oz/50 g
Watercress	20 cups/5 L	8 oz/250 g

Acknowledgments

Don Lynch, historian of the Titanic Historical Society, who knows more than anyone about the *Titanic*'s passengers, provided much of the color that found its way into the text. James Lowe, Graham Wignall, and Jeff Dinan shared their memories of luxury liner life behind the scenes and belowdecks. Dave McMunn's elaborate annual *Titanic* dinner was the primary inspiration for "Choreographing a *Titanic* Dinner." James Morris, director of the Stratford Chefs School and proprietor of Rundles Restaurant, helped me navigate the arcane waters of Edwardian culinary practice. Marian Fowler provided insight into Edwardian fashion. Ed and Karen Kamuda of the Titanic Historical Society responded with their customary speed to every request for assistance. And for my first annual *Titanic* Memorial Dinner, Stuart Cotter acted as sous chef, then joined Rick Feldman, Keith Fleming, Kristoff Malencky, John Wallace, and Denis Weil in consuming and complimenting the result.

— **Rick Archbold**

Ladles of thanks to Susan Van Hezewijk, who carefully tested each recipe until it was perfect. And gratitude to my husband, Martin Kouprie, as well as to Doug, Jeanne, and Vincent McCauley, for their unwavering enthusiasm and encouragement for my culinary pursuits.

— **Dana McCauley**

Three fine editors worked with us on this project: Hugh Brewster conceived the idea and helped us refine it along the way, Mireille Majoor performed her usual magic as the substantive editor and skillfully shepherded the book through every stage of production, and Laurie Coulter conducted a masterful copy edit of a very complicated text.

— **Rick Archbold and Dana McCauley**

Madison Press Books would like to thank Ken Marschall, for sharing his vast knowledge of the *Titanic* as well as his extensive picture collection; Raymond H. Lepien for providing material from his collection; The Titanic Historical Society; Mr. and Mrs. George A. Fenwick; Joy and Fred Norton; and Rosemary Hillary.

PHOTOGRAPH AND ILLUSTRATION CREDITS

Every effort has been made to correctly attribute all the material reproduced in this book. If any errors have unwittingly occurred, we will be happy to correct them in future editions.

Cover: Albert Chevalier Tayler (1862-1925). *An Elegant Soirée.* Fine Art Photographic Library.
Back Cover: (top) Paul Chabas (1869-1937). *The Corner of the Table.* Musée des Beaux-Arts, Tourcoing. Giraudon/ Bridgeman Art Library. (bottom) Titanic Historical Society.
1: Ken Marschall Collection.
2-3: "Guests arrive for a banquet at the Savoy." *London's Social Calendar,* 1912. Mary Evans Picture Library.
4-5: *The Shipbuilder.*

7: Joseph Marius Avy (1871-1939). *Souvenir d'un Soir.* Musée de Roubaix, France. Giraudon/Bridgeman Art Library.
8: The Bettmann Archive.
10: Mary Evans Picture Library.
12-13: "Dining at the Berkeley Restaurant." *Illustrated London News,* 1912. Mary Evans Picture Library.
14: Ulster Folk and Transport Museum, Northern Ireland.
15: (top left) *Illustrated London News;* (bottom left) Don Lynch Collection; (right) Private Collection.
16: Titanic Historical Society.
17: (top) Brown Brothers; (bottom) Don Lynch Collection.

18: (left) Brown Brothers; (right) *Cork Examiner.*
19: Onslow's Auctioneers.
20: (top) Titanic Historical Society; (bottom right) Ken Marschall Collection; (bottom left) Onslow's Auctioneers.
23: (left) Brown Brothers; (right) "Fashionable Ladies." *Le Rire,* 1909. Mary Evans Picture Library.
24: (left) "The morning tea tray." *Every Woman's Encyclopedia,* 1911. Mary Evans Picture Library; (right) Private Collection.
25: (left) Titanic Historical Society; (right) Archibald James Stuart Wortley (1849-1905). *Edward VII.* Forbes Magazine Collection. Bridgeman Art Library.

26: (top) Facsimile menu courtesy Titanic Historical Society; (bottom) *Illustrated London News.*
27: Ken Marschall Collection.
28: Ulster Folk and Transport Museum, Northern Ireland.
31: Peter Miller. *Palm Court — Winter at the Ritz.* Private Collection. Bridgeman Art Library.
32: (top) The New York Public Library; (bottom) *Illustrated London News.*
33: (top) *Illustrated London News;* (bottom) Ken Marschall Collection.
35: Paul Chabas (1869-1937). *The Corner of the Table.* Musée des Beaux-Arts, Tourcoing. Giraudon/Bridgeman Art Library.

37: Ulster Folk and Tranport Museum, Northern Ireland.

38: Ken Marschall Collection.

39: Jean François Raffaelli (1850-1924). *Fleurs, Fruits et Champagne*. Fine Art Photographic Library Ltd./Waterhouse & Dodd.

40: (top) Ken Marschall Collection; (bottom) Private Collection.

41: (all) Ken Marschall Collection.

42: Albert Chevalier Tayler (1862-1925). *An Elegant Soirée* (detail). Fine Art Photographic Library.

43: Ken Marschall Collection.

44: (all) Photography by Ken Marschall.

45: (all) Titanic Historical Society.

46: (left, top right) Raymond H. Lepien Collection; (bottom) Ken Marschall Collection.

47: Southampton City Heritage Services.

48: "A four-glass affair." *Le Journal Amusant*, 1901. Mary Evans Picture Library.

51: "Chefs at work." *L'illustration*, 1893. Mary Evans Picture Library.

55: "Supper at the Savoy, London." *London's Social Calendar*, 1912. Mary Evans Picture Library.

57: "Dessert." 1907. Mary Evans Picture Library.

58: Eloise Harriet Stannard (1829-1915). *A Basket of Oranges*. Ackermann and Johnson Ltd., London. The Bridgeman Art Library.

59: Brown Brothers.

60: "Ball supper in the Salon de Verdure, the Savoy." *London's Social Calendar*, 1912. Mary Evans Picture Library.

61: Byron Collection, Museum of the City of New York.

62-63: Private Collection.

64: (all) Ken Marschall Collection.

65: (top) Byron Collection, Museum of the City of New York; (bottom left and right) Ken Marschall Collection.

66: (top) Ken Marschall Collection; (bottom) Private Collection.

68: The Father Browne S. J. Collection/Ken Marschall Collection.

69: Ken Marschall Collection.

71: Ken Marschall Collection.

72: Eugene Boudin (1824-1898). *Still Life with Oysters*. City of Bristol Museum and Art Gallery. The Bridgeman Art Library.

73: "Soups" (detail). *Mrs. Beeton's Household Management*, 1907. Mary Evans Picture Library.

74: "A dinner party in high society." *La Vie Parisienne*, 1908. Mary Evans Picture Library.

76: Ken Marschall Collection.

78: Onslow's Auctioneers.

85: "Supper buffet." *Mrs. Beeton's Household Management*, 1907. Mary Evans Picture Library.

87: Eloise Harriet Stannard (1829-1915). *Still Life of Fruit on a Marble Ledge*. Bonhams, London. The Bridgeman Art Library.

91: "Cigars." *Simplicissimus*, 1915. Mary Evans Picture Library.

94: Ken Marschall Collection.

95: Private Collection.

96: Ken Marschall Collection.

97: Facsimile menu courtesy Titanic Historical Society.

98: North Wind Picture Archives.

99: *A page from Mrs. Beeton's Cookbook on Fish* (detail). The Bridgeman Art Library.

103: *A Selection of Christmas Puddings* (detail). Warne's Model Cookery and Housekeeping Book, illustrated by Kronheim, 1869. The Bridgeman Art Library.

104: Joseph Seboth (1814-1883). *A Still Life of Fruit*. Fine Art Photographic Library Ltd./Colin Stodgell.

107: "The Pillared Room." 1910. Mary Evans Picture Library.

108: (left) Ken Marschall Collection; (right) North Wind Picture Archives.

109: (top) *The Shipbuilder*; (bottom left and right) Ken Marschall Collection.

110: Ken Marschall Collection.

111: Ken Marschall Collection.

112: Private Collection.

113: National Maritime Museum.

114: (all) Titanic Historical Society.

115: Alfred Hirv. *Still Life with Cauliflower*, 1916. Estonian Art Museum, Tallinn. The Bridgeman Art Library.

117: Courtesy of Mr. and Mrs. George A. Fenwick.

118: North Wind Picture Archives.

119: Ken Marschall Collection.

121: Ken Marschall Collection.

SUGGESTED READING

🐦 Ballard, Robert D. with Rick Archbold. *The Discovery of the Titanic*. New York: Warner Books, 1995. London: Orion, 1995. Toronto: Penguin, 1995.

🐦 Booth, John and Sean Coughlan. *Titanic: Signals of Disaster*. Westbury, Wilts.: White Star Publications, 1993.

🐦 Eaton, John P. and Charles A. Haas. *Titanic: Triumph and Tragedy*. New York, London: W.W. Norton & Company, 1986.

🐦 Hyslop, Donald, Alistair Forsyth and Sheila Jemima. *Titanic Voices*. Southampton: Oral History, City Heritage, Southampton City Council, 1994.

🐦 Lord, Walter. *The Illustrated A Night to Remember*. New York: Holt, Rinehart & Winston, 1976.

🐦 ——. *The Night Lives On*. New York: William Morrow and Company, Inc. 1986.

🐦 Lynch, Don and Ken Marschall. *Titanic: An Illustrated History*. New York: Hyperion, 1992. London: Hodder & Stoughton, 1992. Toronto: Penguin, 1992.

🐦 Marcus, Geoffrey. *The Maiden Voyage*. London: George Allen & Unwin, Ltd. 1969.

🐦 Maxtone-Graham, John. *The Only Way to Cross*. New York: Macmillan Publishing Company, 1972.

🐦 *Ocean Liners of the Past: The White Star Triple Screw Atlantic Liners Olympic and Titanic*. Cambridge: Patrick Stephens, 1983.

🐦 Wade, Wyn Craig. *The Titanic: End of a Dream*. New York: Rawson, Wade Publishers, Inc., 1979.

🐦 Williamson, Ellen. *When We Went First Class*. Iowa State University Press, 1990.

All issues of **The Titanic Commutator**, *published by the Titanic Historical Society (P.O. Box 51053, Indian Orchard, Massachussets, 01151-0053, U.S.A.) are an invaluable resource.*

General Index

Recipe Index

*Design, Typography and
Art Direction:*
 Gordon Sibley
 Design Inc.

Editorial Director:
 Hugh Brewster

Project Editor:
 Mireille Majoor

Production Director:
 Susan Barrable

Production Coordinator:
 Donna Chong

Color Separations:
 Colour Technologies

Printing and Binding:
 Butler & Tanner Limited

LAST DINNER ON THE TITANIC
was produced by Madison Press Books, which is under the direction of
ALBERT E. CUMMINGS

Hosting a *Titanic* Dinner

Jules Alexandre Grun (1868-1934), *The End of Dinner*, 1913. Musée des Beaux-Arts, Tourcoing. Giraudon/Bridgeman Art Library

"Those meals!
Those endless, extravagant meals, in which they
all indulged all year round!"

— Vita Sackville-West, on Edwardian dining

Invitations

To SET THE TONE FOR A PROPER EDWARDIAN SOCIAL EVENING, SEND your guests formal, handwritten invitations. The replies should also be handwritten and follow the exact form of the invitation being accepted. Using the White Star Line logo on the invitations will give them just the right flavor. Send the invitations well in advance (six weeks or more). This will give both you and your guests ample time to prepare. Once you've received your acceptances, the next step is to provide all the information your guests will need to make the evening a success.

Several weeks before your party, mail a package with a letter explaining any ground rules you have established (period costume, assigning specific characters) and setting the scene for the party. Include reading suggestions (see *Suggested Reading*); period costume ideas (see *What to Wear*); and biographies of the passengers the guests are being asked to play (see *Table Talk on the Titanic*). For a modest cost, the Titanic Historical Society can provide a facsimile White Star Line brochure and a facsimile booklet containing the names of all the first- and second-class passengers on the *Titanic*.

The White Star luggage sticker (top), logo (above), and first-class menu cover (opposite) can be copied onto your own invitations, place cards, and menus.

If you want to engender an even greater sense of expectation, you might consider following the lead of one of the several annual *Titanic* dinners we know of and re-create the experience of actually preparing for a transatlantic crossing:

Four weeks before the dinner: Send your guests the facsimile White Star brochure from 1911, describing the various shipboard accommodations and prices.

Three weeks before the dinner: Mail out tickets, luggage tags, and deck card facsimiles. (The deck card indicates on which deck their cabin is located.) Fill out the ticket indicating how many cubic feet of luggage each passenger is carrying, the number of servants allowed, etc. Include, as well, information about the boat train from London, or, if the passenger is departing from Cherbourg, the train from Paris.

One week before the dinner: Send out the passenger list and any final instructions.

EUROPA

COLUMBIA

R.M.S. TITANIC RESTAURANT RECEPTION ROOM

What to Wear

"THE SCENE MIGHT HAVE BEEN IN London or New York," wrote passenger Helen Candee, "with the men in evening dress, the women shining in pale satins and clinging gauze. The prettiest girl even wore a glittering frock of dancing length, with silver fringe around her dainty white satin feet." As Mrs. Candee's recollection indicates, for the women, the range of possibilities was considerably wider than for the men, for whom formal evening clothes remain much the same to this day. (The

The hourglass silhouette so favored by fashionable Edwardian ladies would have been impossible to achieve without the assistance of tightly laced corsets and strategic padding. Male evening dress, on the other hand, has changed relatively little from the *Titanic*'s day.

(all) Mary Evans Picture Library

"prettiest girl" she refers to is herself.) Floor-length dresses were definitely the norm. According to *Vogue: History of 20th Century Fashion* by Jane Mulvagh, in 1911, hemlines "returned to just two inches above the ground. The hem width of skirts designed for the average figure did not exceed two and half yards, allowing just enough fullness to walk."

Ulster Folk and Tranport Museum, Northern Ireland

Creating the Atmosphere

ONE HOST WE KNOW HANGS A BRASS plate engraved with the words "First-Class Entrance" on his front door, his way of announcing to his guests that when they cross the threshold they are stepping back in time to the Edwardian era. If your guests arrive in period dress, they will undoubtedly find it easier to assume their roles if they adopt the formal tone that would have characterized an Edwardian social evening. According to *The London Ritz Book of Etiquette*,  "there have never been as many rules regarding manners and etiquette as existed during the Victorian and Edwardian eras."

Here are a few helpful hints. Whenever a lady rises, or enters or leaves the room, all of the gentlemen automatically stand up. Unless guests are on terms of intimate acquaintance, they address each other as Mr., Miss or Mrs. An exact balance of men and women is desirable, since each lady will be escorted to the table by a specific gentleman. When these two are introduced in the reception room before dinner, the gentleman bows to the lady, but never shakes her hand. When the whole party moves to the dining room, the host leads the way with the most important lady on his arm; the hostess enters last, escorted by the most distinguished gentleman.

Setting the Table

The richly arranged table seen above shows
off the shaded candles, personalized placecards,
and tiny dishes of nuts, olives, and sweets typical
of Edwardian settings. For your own *Titanic* dinner
we suggest the following arrangement:
A. side plate; B. large fork; C. dessert fork;
D. napkin; E. cheese knife; F. dessert spoon;
G. dinner knife; H. soup spoon; I. glass
for champagne or sparkling wine; J. wineglass
(white); K. wineglass (red).

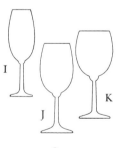

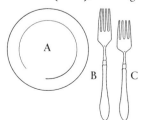

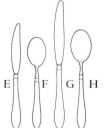

IN THE À LA CARTE REST-
aurant that night, Mrs.
Walter Douglas remem-
bered the flowers, especially the
bouquets of American Beauty
roses. In the first-class dining
room, big bowls of fresh fruit
adorned every table.

How elaborate your place
settings are will depend on how
fancy you want to be, what you
own (or can borrow), and how
many courses you intend to
serve. But bring out your best
china, crystal, and silver.

No record exists of the
intimate lighting for the *Titanic*'s
tables. Original plans called for
shaded electric lamps in the à la
carte restaurant, but the deco-
rators must have changed their
minds. To enhance the atmosphere in appropriately Edwardian fashion, use candles with
lampshades. Each shade sits on
a follower, which "follows" the
candle as it burns down. A
definitely authentic touch is
to cut the butter into a five-
pointed star, the emblem of
the White Star Line.

Each diner would have
found a menu card sitting at his

or her place, and likely each man would have found a red carnation boutonniere supplied by Bealing of Southhampton. This firm provided the profusion of flowers, potted palms, and ferns in the public rooms, causing one passenger to remark that the *Titanic* was "a ship full of flowers." If your guests are assuming the roles of specific passengers, place a printed card with the passenger's name at each place.

Napkin Folding

Elaborately folded napkins are a feature of period photographs of the *Titanic*'s dining rooms. To create the Bishop's Miter for your own table, begin with a large—at least 24 x 24 inch—starched linen napkin.

1) Fold the napkin into thirds as shown.

2) Bring the left edge and the right edge to the center of the folded napkin.

3) Complete the folds so that the outer edges meet in the middle.

4) Bring the lower right-hand corner to the center in an angled fold.

5) Repeat with the upper left-hand corner.

6) Pick up the napkin and fold it away from you along its center so that A1 meets A2 and B1 meets B2. Bring the left-hand corner toward you.

7) Tuck the left-hand corner behind the front triangle formed by A1 and B1.

8) Fold the right-hand corner away from you and tuck it behind the back triangle formed by A2 and B2. The Bishop's Miter is now complete.

Illustration by Jack McMaster

Table Talk on the *Titanic*

T O MAKE YOUR RE-CREATION OF THE LAST DINNER ON THE *TITANIC* COMPLETE, YOU AND YOUR guests may wish to assume the roles of some of the famous—and not-so-famous—diners. To give you several options, we've chosen tables from both the à la carte restaurant and the first-class dining saloon, given you brief biographies for all the *dramatis personae* and any interesting information we know about their relationships. After that, it's up to your imagination.

The à la carte Restaurant

The Widener Dinner Party

O F ALL THE DINING GROUPS ON THE *TITANIC* that night, the Widener dinner party is the most famous. For here sat Captain Smith, gossiping with these scions of society while his ship steamed full ahead into a field of ice. The presence of Captain Smith ensured that the wonders of the brand-new *Titanic* and its performance on the maiden voyage occupied a good portion of the meal. If the topic of icebergs was raised, Marian Thayer didn't hear it. According to her, "Mr. Widener, Major Butt and I were deeply engrossed in conversation on other subjects during the entire time of the dinner."

GEORGE DUNTON WIDENER
❦

Widener presided over one of the greatest fortunes in America, but he would never be a wholly accepted member of Philadelphia Society, which looked down its collective nose at such relative parvenus as the members of New York's fabled Four Hundred. Peter Widener, George's father, had begun his working life as a butcher's apprentice, and neither fortune nor a house full of Rembrandts and Van Dycks would ever completely obliterate his proletarian origins. According to his nephew Arrell, George "was a lot like Grandfather," whose familial kindliness was balanced with ruthless business acumen. And George had his father's "understanding of people," which stood him in good stead as he increasingly assumed the reins of the senior Widener's business empire.

ELEANOR ELKINS WIDENER
❦

Known as Nellie to her friends, she was the daughter of William Elkins, Peter Widener's long-

time business partner and co-founder of his street railway empire. Her nephew Arrell remembered her as slightly plump—no Gibson girl—but with a face "full of good humor and energy" and possessing a "brittle wit."

In Paris she had bought a dress for her daughter Eleanor—"Dimple" to her intimates—whose wedding was planned for June. The dress was trimmed with old family lace Nellie had carried with her for the purpose. Despite the deaths of her father and her elder brother in the sinking, Dimple's wedding went ahead as planned.

HARRY WIDENER

His biographical entry in *The National Cyclopedia of American Biography* describes the Widener heir simply as a "bibliophile." Indeed, the acquisition of rare and beautiful books and manuscripts was so much this young man's obsession that he had traveled to Europe solely for the opportunity to purchase the rare edition of Bacon's *Essays* he carried with him to his watery grave. In fact, his last words were, "Mother, I have placed the volume in my pocket; little 'Bacon' goes with me." He left behind him one of the finest collections of the works of Charles Dickens and Robert Louis Stevenson in American hands. In his memory, his mother endowed the Harry Elkins Widener Memorial Library at Harvard University, from which he had graduated in 1907.

MAJOR ARCHIBALD W. BUTT

In 1912, forty-six-year-old Archie Butt was at the peak of his career. First as military aide to President Theodore Roosevelt, then as aide to President William Taft, he had become accustomed to moving in the highest circles of power and society. His usefulness at official functions was by now legendary. At a reception given for the leading members of America's judiciary, he presented an incredible 1,275 people to President Taft in a single hour.

But recently the bachelor who had everything had found himself in an impossible position. His old friend Roosevelt had announced that he would run against Taft in the upcoming presidential election, splitting the Republican Party and Major Butt's loyalties. The difficulty of choosing between his two friends and mentors had left Archie on the verge of a nervous breakdown. Hence his lengthy sojourn in Europe.

JOHN BORLAND THAYER II

John Thayer's job as second vice president of the Pennsylvania Railroad had so worn him out that he had taken an extended leave of absence to recuperate, a situation that may have given him particular empathy for Major Butt's travails. Although born into an established Philadelphia

family, Thayer had risen to his current position the hard way. He had left school at age nineteen to join the railway and had started his career at the Pennsylvania Railroad as a freight clerk. His success allowed him to build a palatial house in Haverford, Pennsylvania. Like so many of the men in first class, Thayer would refuse to enter the lifeboat that carried his wife to safety, believing in the dictum, "Ladies and children first."

MARIAN LONGSTRETH MORRIS THAYER

We know little about Marian Thayer, except that she was a proper Philadelphia lady. Among the accounts of survivors, nothing she said or did on April 14 is mentioned except for a long stroll on deck with her dear friend Emily Ryerson, whose son had just been killed in a car crash. She would lose her husband when the *Titanic* went down, but her son Jack, Jr. (John B. Thayer III) leapt from the sinking ship and swam to safety.

WILLIAM ERNEST CARTER

If ever someone could be said to have been born with a silver spoon in his mouth, it would be Billy Carter, son by a second marriage to a Philadelphia industrialist whose fortune was built on coal and iron. In fact, Billy's father had played a role in the formation of the Philadelphia Street Railway, the business that had made George Widener's father so wealthy. Undoubtedly the two had known each other since boyhood. An excellent horseman, Billy had made polo, the sport of aristocrats, his game: he played for the Bryn Mawr Benedicts. Indeed, at least one source suggests that Mr. Carter's polo ponies, having accompanied him to England, went down with the *Titanic*. A true cosmopolite, he divided his time between Europe and America, where he enjoyed a prominent position in Philadelphia Society, a position not helped however, when he became one of the few men in first class to survive the sinking.

LUCILLE POLK CARTER

Her lineage was thoroughbred, but this Baltimore debutante definitely made a step up the social ladder when she married William Carter in 1896. Apparently Mrs. Carter cut a vivacious and stylish figure, "with her hourglass figure and Gibson Girl hair," according to one commentator. She wasn't afraid to shock her peers with "the most bizarre modes of the moment," to quote a contemporary newspaper account. She was the first woman in Philadelphia to wear a harem skirt. Later "she created a sensation at Newport when she appeared at a costume ball, given by Mrs. Stuyvesant Fish, in the guise of a fairy, with filmy costume and gauzy wings." No doubt at dinner that evening she was wearing the most daring mode of the moment, fresh from a shopping spree in Paris.

In early 1914, she divorced her husband and shocked Society yet again when later the same year she secretly married another prominent Philadelphian, George Brooke. Was the divorce caused by a secret affair or the shame of being married to a man who had survived the sinking?

CAPTAIN EDWARD J. SMITH

The *Titanic*'s commanding officer exuded self-confidence and charm. As White Star's commodore of the line, he was the inevitable choice to command the world's greatest ship on her maiden voyage. Then he would retire, having pocketed yet another bonus—this effectively doubled his salary, which was already twice that of the best paid Cunarder. So popular was Smith with his wealthy passengers that travel plans were made around the schedule of his personal sailings. In fact, he was known as the millionaires' captain, as at ease with men like John Jacob Astor and Ben Guggenheim as he was with his own officers. The evening of the last dinner, Smith was at the pinnacle of his career. No wonder he lingered a bit longer than perhaps he should

have over that last cigar in the company of these rich and important people. Catering to their tastes and basking in their approval had gotten him where he was.

The Harrises and the Futrelles

The liveliest table in the à la carte restaurant that night must surely have been that occupied by the Harrises and the Futrelles. René Harris and May Futrelle were having a wonderful time on board the *Titanic* and this was the most glittering evening of a glittering voyage. They and their husbands were no strangers to glamour: Jacques Futrelle was a famous novelist and journalist; Henry Harris was one of the top Broadway producers of his day.

HENRY BURKHARDT HARRIS

In *The Maiden Voyage*, Geoffrey Marcus describes Harris as "a well-nourished individual of forty-six, who was prominent in the New York theatrical world and had a number of plays running in the metropolis and on tour. He was returning with a British play which he hoped would be a success on Broadway." Harris was one of the most successful American theatrical producers of the period, even owning a popular Broadway theater, the Hudson, on West Forty-third Street. So successful was he that his wife sued the White Star Line for $1 million in compensation after her husband's loss.

Cork Examiner

RENÉ HARRIS

That Mrs. Harris used the masculine form for her first name suggests both an ignorance of the French language and a background considerably inferior to most of the diners in the Ritz Restaurant that night. Regardless of her origins, however, here was a woman of tremendous spunk. Just before dinner she slipped and fell on the grand staircase, breaking her arm. But Dr. Henry Frauenthal of New York, a joint specialist who happened to be on board, set it in her stateroom, she dressed for dinner—in a sleeveless gown—and made a dramatic entrance, despite "suffering torture." Fellow passengers clustered around her in sympathy. Captain Smith, on his way to the Widener party, paused to compliment her on her spirit. The reception "made me feel that a broken arm was an asset," she later wrote.

After losing her husband, she needed all the spunk she could muster. Having to settle for a final compensation of $50,000—far less than the $1 million she had claimed—she took over her husband's business, a rare event in those days. As the first woman producer on Broadway, she had a knack for nurturing actors and backed *The Beloved Bandit*, the first play by a young playwright named Moss Hart.

JACQUES FUTRELLE

While a young reporter for the Atlanta *Journal*, Jacques Futrelle wrote his first short story starring the brilliantly analytical academic turned detective, Professor S.F.X. Van Dusen, known as "The Thinking Machine." But it was not until many years later, in October 1905, when Futrelle was working for Hearst's recently established *Boston American*, that Professor Van Dusen reached the public. The first story was an instant success and many more followed, helping the paper's rapid rise in circulation. By 1912, Futrelle was a household name and could well afford to travel in style. He must have relished the sobriquet "the American Sherlock Holmes," since Conan Doyle's famous sleuth had been his boyhood idol.

LILY MAY PEEL FUTRELLE

Like Mrs. Harris, May Futrelle seems to have been having the time of her life. In her account of the disaster published soon after the sinking, she describes the atmosphere that evening in rhapsodic terms. "It was a brilliant crowd. Jewels flashed from the gowns of the women. And, oh, the dear women, how fondly they wore their latest Parisian gowns," she gushed. "The soft sweet odor of flowers pervaded the atmosphere. I remember at our table, there was a great bunch of American Beauty roses. . . There was such an atmosphere of fellowship and delightful sociability which makes dinner on the Sabbath on board ship a delightful occasion."

The First-Class Dining Saloon

The Purser's Table

IN THE CENTER OF THE FIRST-CLASS DINING saloon was a large oval table presided over by Hugh McElroy, the ship's chief purser. The table seated ten to twelve, more than any other in the room, but we have reliable evidence for only two of the passengers who sat there regularly—William T. Stead and Frederic Seward. A third, Mrs. Henry B. Cassebeer, almost certainly took her meals there as well. Since we can be sure that the genial and popular McElroy liked to surround himself with a fascinating mix of people, we have placed some of the richest or most interesting of the first-class diners into the unassigned seats. Use this "millionaires' table" as your model if you're planning to serve the many-course meal from first class to a large group of friends.

HUGH B. MCELROY
~

Like Captain Smith, Hugh McElroy was so popular with White Star's well-heeled customers that some would sail only on his ships. Passengers remembered him as cutting a tall, commanding figure and having diplomatic skills that allowed him to deal with the most difficult of passengers. But it was the twinkle in his eye and his wonderful sense of humor that caused travelers to vie for a seat at his table.

Where Captain Smith seems to have gone into shock after the iceberg hit, Purser McElroy rose to the occasion. His was one of the few figures of calm and authority that passengers remembered as they boarded the lifeboats.

WILLIAM T. STEAD
~

Although Stead was indisposed on the evening of April 14 and so took dinner in his stateroom, he will make a delightful addition to your *Titanic* dinner party—if you are willing to stretch the rules a little. At sixty-two, Stead had lost some of the fire that had made him into a pioneering, crusading journalist and one of the most powerful opinion-makers of the late Victorian era. But he was apparently in fine form on the maiden voyage, a captivating conversationalist with strong views and a trunkful of fascinating anecdotes from his long career.

When he was at the table, conversation ranged from politics to history to spiritualism, a thirty-year obsession. Apparently, he claimed to be in touch on a regular basis with a spirit guide named Julia. Despite this unconventional side, he retained such admiration on both sides of the Atlantic that President Taft had invited him to address a peace conference on April 21 at New York's Carnegie Hall.

FREDERIC KIMBER SEWARD

Fred Seward, a respected New York corporate lawyer, was returning from a business trip to Greece. He sat next to William Stead and found the great journalist fascinating. Seward was the son of a minister and a devoted alumnus of Columbia University. One of the relatively few first-class men who were saved, Seward stepped reluctantly into lifeboat No. 7, which was ready to leave the ship but only partly filled. Among his boatmates were Dorothy Gibson and her mother, Pauline.

DOROTHY GIBSON

In 1912, motion pictures were in their infancy and movie actresses were nothing like the celebrities they are today. Dorothy was associated with Eclair Motion Pictures and her photo had appeared in *Billboard Magazine* in 1911. In fact, few people on board seem to have realized that Dorothy Gibson, a seemingly proper young woman traveling with her mother, was a professional model and minor movie star. One wonders if even her mother knew that Dorothy's enjoyment of the maiden voyage was immeasurably improved when she received a wireless message from Jules Brulatour, a wealthy and very married backer of motion pictures. She and Jules were in love and his telegram made her "awfully happy." Alas, this happiness was not to last much beyond their eventual marriage in 1917. But after the divorce Dorothy managed to walk away with a tidy $10,000 a year in alimony.

MRS. PAULINE GIBSON

We know little of this shadowy figure, Dorothy Gibson's mother, beyond her first name and the fact that she was married to a Mr. Leonard Gibson.

MRS. GENEVIEVE CASSEBEER

Walter Lord tells us that Mrs. Henry B. Cassebeer was "an impecunious young widow, but a very experienced traveler." Apparently, she managed to persuade the purser's office to upgrade her ticket from second class to first class—perhaps a few pounds changed hands—and then to charm the chief purser into seating her at his table. Presumably McElroy enjoyed the company of an attractive young woman and thought she would add leaven to a mix that included intellectual heavyweights like Stead.

JOHN JACOB ASTOR

The richest man on board, Astor was the great-grandson of a poor south German immigrant who had founded the family fortune in the early nineteenth-century fur trade. Subsequent generations had only increased the Astor wealth, mostly through adroit investments in real estate. As a result of his vast inherited wealth, John Jacob Astor could do pretty much what he pleased. One commentator of the day described him as "the world's greatest monument to unearned increment." He was accustomed to getting his own way, but he seemed to have gone too far when he divorced his first wife in 1909 then remarried a young woman of eighteen two years later. This serious social sin had put at risk his position as one of the leaders of New York Society.

MADELINE FORCE ASTOR

New York Society was unlikely to be thrilled by the return of the new Mrs. Astor, barely nineteen and now visibly pregnant after a winter in Egypt and on the Continent. After losing her first husband on the *Titanic*, she would remarry, but her life was to be a shorter one than his. She died at age forty-six.

BENJAMIN GUGGENHEIM

The eldest of the seven sons of Meyer Guggenheim, a Swiss immigrant who reportedly began his financial rise selling shoelaces on Philadelphia streets, Benjamin Guggenheim had presided over a considerable expansion of the family's fortune. According to Geoffrey Marcus, the Guggenheims formed "one of the most closely knit family businesses the United States had ever seen." But in 1911, Ben had broken away to go into business on his own and was apparently suffering embarrassing financial losses.

"Our Coterie"—Archibald Gracie's Table

MRS. HELEN CANDEE HAD NOT BEEN assigned to the table where Colonel Archibald Gracie, Edward Kent, and Clinch Smith sat, but by the fourth day of the voyage these men in late middle age had become part of her circle. She might very well have sat at the empty fourth place in order to avoid her own table, which she found uncongenial. "Our coterie," as Archibald Gracie described this group, included Hugh Woolner, the son of a famous English sculptor, and Bjornstrom Steffanson, a handsome young Swedish businessman whose family fortune came from wood pulp. "Together, they formed one of those groups that sometimes happens on an Atlantic crossing," writes Walter Lord in *The Night Lives On*, "where the chemistry is just right and the members are inseparable."

HELEN CHURCHILL CANDEE

A woman of a certain age, but no uncertain handsomeness and charm, Helen Candee managed to thoroughly enjoy the voyage despite the fact that her son Harry had been injured in an airplane crash, her reason for returning from Europe ahead of schedule. A woman of good breeding and impeccable social standing, Mrs. Candee was nonetheless somewhat ahead of her time. She already had two books to her credit, including a volume called *How Women May Earn a Living*; her latest tome was scheduled for fall publication.

COLONEL ARCHIBALD GRACIE

Gregarious and well bred, of military bearing and manner, Colonel Gracie must have been a bit of a bore, albeit a genial and likable one. Although he was returning from a trip to Europe designed to help him recover from the decidedly lukewarm reviews of his mammoth labor, *The Truth About Chickamauga*, he was having such a good time that he had completely neglected his usually strict regimen of physical exercise. Only on Sunday morning did he finally visit the ship's gymnasium. "I enjoyed myself as if I were in a summer palace at the seashore, surrounded with every comfort," he wrote of the *Titanic*'s maiden voyage.

Gracie owed his personal wealth to his success selling real estate, not to his rather unremarkable military career. It was this money that had provided the leisure to research the Civil War battle of Chickamauga for seven years. But it was his connection to an old southern family—his father had roomed with Robert E. Lee at West Point—that made him feel so at ease with the Strauses, the Astors, and the Wideners—people considerably wealthier than he.

JAMES CLINCH SMITH

Noted for his deadpan humor, Clinch Smith was returning from Paris where he had persuaded his estranged wife, Bertha, to agree to a reconciliation. Mrs. Candee remembered him as "a gentle, slow paced man." By profession, he seems to have been a socialite. He kept a house in Paris and another on Long Island, where he housed his polo ponies, and moved between them at his leisure. According to a recent biography of his brother-in-law, famed architect Stanford White, his family belonged to "authentic New York gentry, allied to such eminent families as the Floyds, the Nicollses, and the Van Cortlands."

EDWARD AUSTIN KENT

Kent had left the United States in early February, pausing first in England, then traveling to the Riviera and thence to Egypt, staying longer than planned so that he could return on the brand-new *Titanic*. A bachelor and prominent Buffalo architect, at fifty-eight he was now contemplating retirement. He and Mrs. Candee had mutual friends, a fact that helped break the ice between them.

"Strange to see how a good dinner and feasting reconciles everybody."

— Samuel Pepys